The Philosophy of Rousseau

RONALD GRIMSLEY

The Philosophy of Rousseau

OXFORD UNIVERSITY PRESS
London   Oxford   New York
1973

Oxford University Press

OXFORD LONDON NEW YORK
GLASGOW TORONTO MELBOURNE WELLINGTON
CAPE TOWN IBADAN NAIROBI DAR ES SALAAM LUSAKA ADDIS ABABA
DELHI BOMBAY CALCUTTA MADRAS KARACHI LAHORE DACCA
KUALA LUMPUR SINGAPORE HONG KONG TOKYO

PRINTED IN GREAT BRITAIN
BY RICHARD CLAY (THE CHAUCER PRESS) LTD
BUNGAY, SUFFOLK

Contents

Biographical Introduction

JEAN-JACQUES ROUSSEAU was born at Geneva on 28 June 1772. As his mother died a few days after his birth, he was brought up for a time by an unstable father, a watchmaker by trade, who gave him no systematic education but taught him to read through the medium of seventeenth-century sentimental novels and Plutarch's *Lives*, works which represented the two ideals—the romantic and the heroic— dominating much of his later life. After being entrusted at the age of ten to a country clergyman, M. Lambercier, and his sister, Rousseau was apprenticed three years later to an engraver who treated him so brutally that in 1728 he decided to leave Geneva to seek his fortune in the world. His first step was to become a Roman Catholic —a decision that was reinforced by the influence of Mme de Warens, another convert, to whom he was sent by the ecclesiastical authorities; Rousseau's emotional dependence on her was to have decisive psychological significance for the rest of his life. After a formal abjuration of Protestantism at the hospice for catechumens at Turin he worked for a time as a lackey in that town; he lost this post when he was accused of the theft of a ribbon, and although he was the real culprit, he tried to put the blame upon a servant girl, Marion, who was dismissed with him. This was an incident for which he felt a life-long guilt. He returned to Mme de Warens at Annecy in 1728. Finding him unsuitable for the priesthood, his ecclesiastical protectors gave him some training as a musician. For a time he travelled rather aimlessly, but in 1731 he rejoined Mme de Warens who was then at Chambéry. A few years later when he was living in rural seclusion at another of Mme de Warens's properties 'Les Charmettes' he set about the task of educating himself through a period of intense study. A brief and unsuccessful experience as private tutor at Lyons in 1740 was followed by a fruitless attempt to persuade the Academy of Sciences at Paris to accept a new system of musical notation. His stay in Paris, however, resulted in a number of introductions to important personages, include Mme Dupin and her son-in-law M. de Francueil. In 1743 he was appointed secretary to M. de Montaigu, the French Ambassador at Venice, but they soon quarrelled and Rousseau was dismissed; in 1744 he went back to Paris, where he became friendly with writers and intellectuals such as Diderot and d'Alembert, the editors of the *Encyclopédie*, to which, later on, he was invited to contribute musical articles as well as an important article on 'Economie politique'. A decisive personal event of this period was his liaison with an illiterate servant girl called Thérèse Levasseur; she bore him five illegitimate children, all of whom were sent to a Foundlings' Home. In later life Rousseau was tormented by feelings of guilt (the full implications of which were never fully acknowledged) over his conduct in this matter.

His first literary work was the *Discours sur les sciences et les arts* which, after winning a prize at the Academy at Dijon in 1749, was published in 1750; it constituted a direct challenge to the social and cultural values of the time in the name of simple virtue and truth. Paradoxically this attack on contemporary society was soon followed by Rousseau's first real success with the performance of his opera, *Le Devin du village*, before Louis XV at Fontainebleau, but his refusal to be presented to the King deprived him of any chance of obtaining favour and financial support. As he became increasingly hostile towards his Parisian environment, he began to turn once again to his native Geneva; in 1754 he made a journey there and was readmitted to Protestantism—an event which, as he admitted, had social and personal rather than truly religious significance, for he had gradually moved away from all forms of Christian orthodoxy. The *Discours sur l'origine de l'inégalité*, which appeared in 1755, represented an important development of his thought, for, starting with man's primitive condition, he sought to trace his subsequent evolution and final fall into depravity and corruption. Feeling more and more unhappy at Paris, he decided to 'reform' his life by renouncing the luxuries of society; accordingly, he accepted an invitation from a friend, Mme d'Epinay, to live in a small country house called 'the Hermitage' at Montmorency. This move was followed by a period of great literary activity and the production of his major works. In 1758 he continued his criticism of contemporary society with his *Lettre à M. d'Alembert sur les spectacles*, in which he vigorously repudiated d'Alembert's suggestion in his *Encyclopédie* article 'Genève', that a theatre should be established in that community; Rousseau saw this as a grave threat to the moral life of his fellow citizens and he linked up his defence of Geneva with a fierce attack upon the theatre in general. Rousseau's personal memories, dreams, and frustrations were responsible for the inception of his novel *La Nouvelle Héloïse* (1761) which began as a story of passion but was soon transformed into a work dealing with moral and religious issues. In the following year appeared one of his most important didactic works, *Émile ou de l'Education*, which was not a mere educational manual but a detailed exposition of Rousseau's philosophy of human nature; it was based on the assumption of man's natural goodness and sought to show how moral corruption originated in the evil influence of contemporary society. Since no education could be complete without a proper understanding of spiritual values, Rousseau included in this work a statement of his religious beliefs in the form of the *Profession de foi du vicaire savoyard*, which, as a defence of natural religion, was mainly responsible for the book's condemnation by the ecclesiastical authorities and the Paris Parlement. Since Rousseau believed that the individual had ultimately to take his place in society, he published in the same year (1762) a systematic statement of his political ideas, *Du Contrat social*, which was merely part of a projected but unfinished work on political institutions; it is a treatise on political right, not a discussion of existing governments, and seeks to grapple with the difficult problem of securing freedom in a society that is both just and human.

This period witnessed a rapid deterioration of Rousseau's relations with the Encyclopedists, and especially Diderot; difficulties were undoubtedly increased by clashes of temperament as well as of principle. The condemnation of *Émile* in 1762 forced Rousseau to flee from France, not simply to escape arrest but also to avoid compromising influential friends who had helped with the publication of the work. He was offered asylum by the King of Prussia who let him settle at Môtiers-Travers in the principality of Neuchâtel. The following year Rousseau delivered a powerful riposte to the Archbishop of Paris's condemnation of *Émile* in the form of a *Lettre à M. de Beaumont*, which is a valuable complement to the more formal presentation of his religious views in the *Profession de foi*. Increasingly opposed to his religious and political ideas, the Genevan authorities finally condemned both *Émile* and the *Contrat social*; this action prompted Rousseau to produce another polemical work, the *Lettres écrites de la Montagne*, in which he criticized the political and religious attitude of Geneva. Local hostility made him feel more and more insecure at Môtiers-Travers, and after stones were thrown at his house in 1765 he went to the Ile de Saint-Pierre where he was extremely happy, but when he was refused permission to stay there, he accepted an invitation from the philosopher David Hume to make his home in England. After a short stay at Chiswick in 1766, Rousseau moved to a large house in Staffordshire. Unfortunately the tensions which, already apparent at the time of the quarrel with Diderot, had been seriously exacerbated by official persecution, began to assume a more intense and irrational form and he soon quarrelled with Hume, whom he accused (quite unjustifiably) of seeking his defamation. Unable to bear the strain any longer, Rousseau fled panic-stricken from England and returned to France in 1767, where he continued to lead an unsettled existence that was haunted by the thought of universal persecution. He married Thérèse Levasseur at Bourgoin in 1768. At last, in 1770, he settled in Paris, where he remained until May 1778, when he moved to the estate of the Marquis de Girardin at Ermenonville; he died there suddenly of apoplexy on 2 July 1778.

During these last years Rousseau's principal literary activity was the production of a series of autobiographical writings—the *Confessions*, to which he devoted considerable time during his stay in England and which he completed after his return to France; the strange dialogues known as *Rousseau juge de Jean-Jacques*, which, in spite of their frequent hysterical tone and pathological content, contain some brilliant pages; the magnificent but unfinished last work, the *Rêveries du Promeneur solitaire*. With these works Rousseau inaugurated a personal and lyrical kind of literature which was to have a remarkable influence through its poetic mood and its sustained effort at self-analysis. The composition of these personal writings was interrupted only by a request to draw up constitutions for Corsica and Poland: the first remained a fairly brief *Projet* but the second (*Sur le gouvernement de Pologne*) was more extensive; both are interesting examples of Rousseau's efforts to apply his general political ideas to particular situations.

The following are Rousseau's principal works:

1750	*Discours sur les sciences et les arts* (composed 1749).
1752	*Le Devin du village* (opera).
	Narcisse (play).
1753	*Lettre sur la musique française* (written 1752).
1755	*Discours sur l'origine de l'inégalité.*
	Économie politique (article in *Encyclopédie*).
1756	*Lettre sur la Providence* (reply to Voltaire's *Poème sur le désastre de Lisbonne*).
1758	*Lettre à d'Alembert sur les spectacles.*
1761	*La Nouvelle Héloïse.*
1762	(Jan.) Composition of four autobiographical letters to Malesherbes.
	Émile.
	Contrat social.
1762	*Lettre à Christophe de Beaumont* (reply to Archbishop's *Mandement* against *Émile*).
1764	*Lettres écrites de la montagne* (reply to J. R. Tronchin's *Lettres écrites de la campagne*).
1765	Composition of *Projet de constitution pour la Corse.*
1766	Composition of first part of *Confessions.*
1767	*Dictionnaire de musique.*
1771–2	Composition of *Considérations sur le gouvernement de Pologne.*
1772–6	Composition of *Dialogues: Rousseau juge de Jean-Jacques.*
1776–8	Composition of *Les Rêveries du promeneur solitaire.*

1

The Function of Philosophy

When in the last years of his life Rousseau reviewed his work as a whole, he insisted upon its essential unity: he claimed to have elaborated an 'interconnected system' which 'might not be true', might even be 'false', but which was 'in no way contradictory (i. 930).[1] He explained the unity of his thought in terms of the constant purpose inspiring it: the development of 'a doctrine which, being as sound as it was simple, and without making any concessions to epicureanism and hypocrisy, was aimed only at the happiness of the human race'. In his very last work he referred to his ideas as forming 'a body of doctrine so solid, so well connected and formed with so much meditation and care' that it was far more convincing than any other philosophical system; his own views expressed 'certain ways of feeling and seeing which distinguished him from all other writers of his time and from most of those who had preceded him' (i. 933). To the Archbishop of Paris, he declared: 'I have written on various subjects, but always with the same principles; always the same morality, the same belief, the same maxims and, if you like, the same opinions' (iv. 928).

At the same time Rousseau was equally adamant in his refusal to call himself a 'philosopher'. 'I am not a great philosopher', he declared in the *Profession de foi*, 'and I have little care to be one. But I sometimes have good sense and I love the truth' (iv. 565). To the Archbishop of Paris who had accused him of not being a philosopher, he replied: 'Agreed! I have never aspired to this title, to which I recognize that I have no right, and I assuredly do not give it up through modesty' (iv. 1004). Not without a trace of irony he described himself to Voltaire as a 'friend of truth who speaks to a philosopher'. To another correspondent he wrote: 'I have never aspired to become a philosopher; I have never claimed to be one; I was not, am not, and do not want to become one.'[2] If he finally elaborated a 'system of ideas', it was as a 'simple, truthful man', not as a professional thinker.

Rousseau did not deny that any thinker, whatever his personal attitude, needed to impose a certain discipline upon his thought and to follow a definite method in the presentation of his ideas. He made this very point in connection with his own works which, he alleged, had been misunderstood because readers had not taken them 'in a certain order'. Yet the true significance of that order and the various divisions (social criticism, moral, religious, and political philosophy) into which he divided the exposition of his ideas still depended upon an adequate comprehension of the fundamental principles inspiring the whole.

These basic principles could not be established by a merely intellectual method. Rousseau's criticism of other philosophers was bound up with the question of the thinker's personal attitude. Whereas, in his opinion, they sought ideas which they could teach to others, he had to have a philosophy that was truly his; the entire emphasis of his thought had been directed towards discovering 'his own true end' (i. 1013); he considered that his intellectual efforts represented 'the most ardent and sincere researches which perhaps have been made by any mortal' (i. 1017). This concern with sincerity made him search for 'fundamental principles accepted by my reason, confirmed by my heart, and which all bear the seal of inner assent in the silence of the passions' (i. 1018). Nevertheless, in Rousseau's opinion, this close connection between philosophical truth and personal sincerity did not lead to the elaboration of a merely subjective outlook; he believed that only a sincere thinker was capable of reaching the truth, and that the personal origin of thought was a guarantee of its objective validity.

Equally important was the thinker's need to recognize that philosophical questions could not be separated from a consideration of man's being as a whole. Rational understanding, though important, depended on something deeper than mere intellect—on an inner determination which chose and loved the truth instead of simply trying to see it. A search for truth limited to intellectual activity alone was bound to be fruitless, since it did not engage the thinker's complete existence; it was only when he penetrated to the depths of his being that he was able to grasp principles which were 'engraved in the human heart in indelible characters' (i. 1021). Through the understanding of his own essential being, the thinker would come to understand the nature of man. This personal attitude thus allowed him to grasp the real features of human—and not merely his own—being and so to move from subjective feeling to the domain of universal principles.

Since philosophy should be concerned primarily with the problem of the 'nature of man', Rousseau believed that his own conception of the philosopher's task was incompatible with the abstract and remote character of traditional metaphysics. In condemning 'this metaphysical deep which has neither bottom nor shape' (ii. 699), he did not differ greatly from those *philosophes* who also claimed to be the enemies of rash system-building; thinkers who had already imbibed the lessons of Locke's empiricism did not need to be reminded of the danger of ignoring the limitations of the human mind. Like his contemporaries, therefore, Rousseau used the term 'metaphysical' in a pejorative sense to describe ideas which were beyond the range of human experience; the philosopher who sought to understand the universe had to acknowledge that the 'insufficiency of his mind' was the primary cause of his intellectual confusion.

We do not have the measure of this huge machine, we cannot calculate its relations; we know neither its first laws nor its final cause; we do not know ourselves; we know neither our nature nor our active principle; we scarcely know whether man is a single or compound being; impenetrable mysteries surround us on all sides; they are above the region of the senses; we think we have the intelligence to penetrate them, but we have only the imagination. (iv. 568)

Although a thinker may be led astray by his overweening intellectual ambition, he must also be on his guard against the opposite danger: that of losing himself in a consideration of isolated facts. As Saint-Preux says in *La Nouvelle Héloïse*, 'each object which strikes the philosopher is considered by him separately; and being able to discern neither its connections nor its relations with other objects which are beyond his reach, he never sees it in its place, and feels neither its reason nor its true effects' (ii. 245–6). If a concern with absolutes is likely to lead the unwary philosopher beyond the confines of attainable knowledge, an exclusive concern with particular facts is equally likely to make him lose sight of the need for establishing guiding principles. Rousseau considered that contemporary philosophers had avoided the dangers of abstract metaphysics only at the cost of falling into the trap of a superficial empiricism limited to the exploration of 'sensations' and likely to produce a soul-destroying materialism. Philosophy, therefore, could not rely on abstract speculation or a narrowly experimental method. Rousseau, as we shall see, was certainly prepared to acknowledge the importance of facts— whether historical, physical, or psychological—but, in his view, they could not exist in their own right, but had to be interpreted in the light of the fundamental principles discovered by sincere personal effort.

Rousseau finds a particularly noteworthy example of this neglect of fundamental principles in the preoccupation of so many contemporary thinkers with 'subtlety'—another word which he almost invariably uses in an unfavourable sense. His insistence on this point is especially significant, for it is related to a psychological, and not merely a philosophical, criticism of traditional metaphysics. By 'subtlety' Rousseau usually means insincerity and wilful mental obtuseness; the elaboration of over-refined distinctions indicates the thinker's refusal to face the need for establishing sound principles. Philosophers do not find truth, because they do not wish to do so; they prefer to make intellectual activity an expression of their own selfish or perverse feelings. 'Even though philosophers were in a position to discover the truth, which of them', asks the Savoyard priest, 'would take an interest in it? Each knows that his system is no more valid than the rest; but he supports it because it is his . . . Where is the one who, in the secrecy of his heart, has any other purpose than to distinguish himself? ... The essential thing is to think differently from the others' (iv. 569). What passes for philosophy is little more than reflection inspired by pride and vanity. This was a point on which Rousseau had insisted from his very first *Discours* onwards. He believed that the search for a philosophical system was poisoned at its very source: the aim of most thinkers was simply to be different from others and to construct a system which would be acknowledged as their own, its truth or falsehood being a matter of little importance. Intellectual subtlety was thus a sign of human perversity.

Rousseau believes that the general effect of this misconception and perversion of philosophical activity is to produce a sharp contradiction between appearance and reality. Admittedly, philosophy here shares one of the most striking features of contemporary life, but it is a particularly serious matter in view of the great esteem in which philosophers are held by so many misguided people! The very persons to whom the untutored turn for enlightenment are precisely the ones most likely to lead them into error and confusion. Perhaps one of the principal causes of this false philosophical attitude which mistakes appearance for reality is the thinker's habit of deluding himself—and others—with words. Here again philosophy merely suffers from a very widespread defect which touches every aspect of modern social life. In his survey of the Parisian scene, for example, Saint-Preux frequently stresses the prevalence of 'verbiage' and 'jargon' in all forms of social activity. In the case of philosophy, however, this abuse of language is especially grave, because it can so easily mislead the thinker into believing that he is affirming truth when he is merely reasoning! How often people are duped by 'this deceptive ostentation which consists only of vain discourse' and 'this futile philosophy which produces mere speechifiers'! (ii. 220, 263c.) Even religious beliefs may be no more than 'a certain jargon of words without ideas, with which people satisfy everything except reason'. The grandiose claims of metaphysics make it especially liable to replace truth by empty words. 'General and abstract truths are the source of man's greatest errors; the jargon of metaphysics has never discovered a single truth and it has filled philosophy with absurdities, of which people are ashamed as soon as they strip them of their big words' (iv. 577).

Instead of losing himself in vain metaphysical abstraction or a bewildering number of isolated facts, the thinker has to start with truths which are intuitively perceived in the depths of his own being. This is what Rousseau himself had been obliged to do: 'Whence', he asks in one of his last works, 'could the painter and apologist of nature, which is today so disfigured and calumnied, have drawn his model save from his own heart?' (i. 936.) When once these principles have beeen discovered, the thinker can develop them by logical reasoning, and deduce certain conclusions from them, but he has first of all to 'withdraw into himself' and 'circumscribe his existence'.

Let us begin by again becoming ourselves, by concentrating ourselves within ourselves, by circumscribing our soul within the same limits as nature has given to our being; let us begin, in a word, by gathering ourselves together where we are, in order that, as we seek to know ourselves, all that constitutes us may come and present itself to us at the same time (iv. 1112).

The exhortation to the thinker to withdraw into himself is also present at the end of the first *Discours* where Rousseau affirms that in order to know the laws of virtue which are 'engraved in every heart', it is enough 'to withdraw into oneself and listen to the voice of one's conscience in the silence of the passions' (iii. 30). As soon as this process of inner withdrawal and concentration has been achieved, the thinker will be in a position to seek the truth, for he will be able to separate 'the first idea of man' from all that is extraneous to him.

Yet Rousseau's insistence on the importance of this initial personal attitude does not mean that he is prepared to discard reason. Its grave misuse by contemporary thinkers in no way impugns its valuable role in the discovery and elaboration of truth. Although Rousseau admitted in his last years that he had 'rarely thought with pleasure, almost always against his will and as it were by force', he also insisted that he had thought 'fairly deeply' (i. 1061). In the very work which stressed his need to find a personal philosophy, he affirmed: 'General and abstract truth is the most precious of all goods; without it, man is blind; it is the eye of reason' (i. 1026). Rousseau was also impelled to assert his belief in the possibility of rational truth because he could not be content to remain a mere sceptic or to live in permanent doubt. To M. de Franquières who had found out that all 'researches on the author of things' resulted in nothing but 'a state of doubt', Rousseau replied: 'I cannot judge of this state, because it has never been mine. In my childhood I believed through authority, in my youth through feeling, and in my maturity through reason; now I believe because I have always believed' (iv. 1134). In this respect he did not think that he was very different from other people. 'Doubt about the things which it is important for it to know, is too violent a state for the human mind; it does not resist for long; it decides somehow or other in spite of itself, and it would rather be mistaken than believe nothing' (iv. 568). Consequently, Rousseau realized that it was not enough to criticize the errors of others; he had to make a serious constructive effort to seek the truth for himself.

Nevertheless, if the philosopher is not to lose himself in vain speculation, it is essential for him to concentrate on truths which 'interest' him and which it is 'important for him to know'. Rousseau does not seem to be using the terms 'interest' and 'importance' in any simple utilitarian or pragmatic sense, but to express the idea of deep personal involvement. Moreover, the sincere thinker cannot remain content with 'appropriating his ideas into his heart', he has also to ensure that they satisfy his reason. Even though he can safely dispense with the 'vain subtlety of arguments', he still has to make an earnest and critical examination of the knowledge which 'interests' him.

Rousseau's efforts to relate certain intuitively perceived truths to the wider problem of human nature and to see this problem within the context of man's being as a whole involve him in the use of reason. Far from denigrating reason, he sometimes praises it so highly that certain modern commentators have not hesitated to speak of his 'rationalism'.[3] Even in a work as heavily charged with emotion as *La Nouvelle Héloïse* reason is described as 'this divine torch' which God has given men for their guidance, while in the *Profession de foi du vicaire savoyard* Rousseau declares that 'all ideas about the deity come from reason alone' (iv. 607). His stress upon the universality of truth also leads him to extol the benefits of reason, since 'reason is common to us all', as the Savoyard priest insists. However, it is at once apparent that the honest thinker's reason is not the reason of thinkers who use it mainly for the elaboration of subtle and insincere arguments. Rousseau is concerned with *la saine raison* or *la raison simple et primitive*, which is one of man's most sublime gifts. As such it can have 'no other aim than what is good' (ii. 370). Sustained by the noblest impulses of the human personality, it enables man to distinguish permanent, universal principles from 'vain sophisms'; through reason he can perceive the truth in 'all the clarity of primitive understanding'. 'Original' or 'primitive' reason is frequently associated in Rousseau's mind with the image of light as well as with the idea of simplicity; it is reason that sheds light on the real nature of relationships which might otherwise be obscured by vague or confused feelings. Here again, however, it is a question of returning to a basic element of human nature, of understanding it in its authentic function, and of accepting it in all its simplicity, clarity, and universality. As soon as ideas are examined *dans le silence des passions*, the most common will also be found to be the simplest, the most reasonable, and the most universal. Whenever Rousseau undertakes a systematic exposition of philosophical ideas, he always emphasizes these particular characteristics. That is why he has such a great admiration for the English deist, Samuel Clarke, whose system he considers to be 'so striking, so luminous, so simple, and it seems to me, offering fewer incomprehensible things to the human mind than the absurd ones that are to be found in any other system' (iv. 570).

One immediate cause of Rousseau's persistent refusal to abandon reason as an instrument of knowledge is its essentially natural character. If all genuine human capacities are good, it would indeed be absurd to eliminate at the outset one of the most striking and effective of them all. Moreover, one of reason's greatest services is to protect man against the tyranny of his fellows by helping him to separate the universal truths available to his own personal inspection from the predominantly irrational opinions imposed upon him by human authority. Many truths, as we have seen, lie beyond reason, but no known truth can ever be against it. Reason is thus a valuable safeguard against tyranny, whether of passion or human will.

Inevitably reason must recognize its limitations as well as its

powers. First of all, it may prove the existence of a reality, the exact
nature of which it is powerless to know. Such is the case with God
and the soul, whose existence can be rationally demonstrated, but
whose ultimate nature lies beyond the range of human intelligence.
If, in certain cases, reason leds us to affirm the existence of a reality
lying beyond it, it would be sheer folly to embark upon a metaphysical exploration of such a mystery. In the second place, reason
is only one essential element in the personality; we must not rashly
assume that it can function in isolation and be the final court of
appeal in all cases of doubt. Certain kinds of feeling, for example,
may in some cases be more reliable guides to truth. Necessary as a
means of attaining clarity and understanding, reason cannot provide
the material for its own activity; it is incapable of supporting itself
on its own foundations. Julie speaks scathingly of 'the vain sophisms
of a reason which relies only on itself' (ii. 359). Cut off from other
human powers, it will remain sterile and ineffective. It may sometimes be wise to acknowledge the importance of impulses lying beyond the range of our immediate reflection. This seems to be the
point of the Vicaire's observation: 'My rule to abandon myself to
feeling rather than to reason is confirmed by reason itself' (iv. 573).
Reason, therefore, cannot provide us with the vital impulse that will
enable us to act decisively in critical situations.

On the other hand, mere feeling, however necessary it may be as an
essential source of action, does not give any explicit awareness of its
ultimate meaning. Even the most exalted feelings must reckon with
their practical effects upon the conduct of life, while in certain cases
the heart may be led astray by wayward passions. In other words,
feelings need to be 'cultivated' in order to give us the 'truth of things',
and reason must play an important part in this educative process. If
feeling enables us to love the good, only reason allows us to know it.
Isolated from the rest of man's powers, reason will undoubtedly fall
into error, but as soon as it is properly related to the self's fundamental needs, its activity is certain to be beneficial.

One particular advantage of reason is that it enables us to perceive
meaningful relations between ourselves and our environment; thanks
to it, we can organize our own inner life and its connection with the
outside world. 'Reason is the faculty of ordering all the faculties of

our soul in accordance with the nature of things and their relations with us' (iv. 1010). In this respect, it is more fundamental than mere reasoning which, as Rousseau goes on to explain, does not help us to know 'primitive truths', but is 'the art of comparing known truths in order to compose from them other truths which one does not know'. In Rousseau's opinion, reason thus has an active quality which is denied to mere 'sensation'; it enables us to make the transition from the 'images' which are simply the mental correlates of the objects of sense, to the domain of 'ideas' which are the 'notions of objects determined by relationships' (iv. 344). Thus when we imagine, we merely see, that is, passively register the impressions of the senses, while thinking involves perceptions and ideas which result from an active process of comparison. Yet the very fact that reason is indispensable to the process of comparison means that it does not function in isolation from the other elements of human experience, for it is 'so to speak only a compound of all other human faculties'—one that develops late and does not take on its full significance until man has reached a certain degree of maturity. The particular expression of reason will evidently depend on the specific stage of human development at which it is functioning—whether, for example, it involves the rudimentary reasoning of the child, or the abstract speculation of the fully grown adult.

In so far as they form part of his general approach to philosophy, Rousseau's views of reason clearly confirm his belief that it is impossible to separate specific philosophical issues from the general problem of human nature and the basic principles which govern all authentic experience. Indeed, an undue narrowing of mental perspective is likely to produce a false view of philosophical problems by separating them from the wider human context to which they properly belong. It is no small part of the philosopher's task to restore the unity of man's 'original' being and to reveal it as it is and not as it merely appears to be. This means that intellectual consistency alone is not an adequate criterion for testing the validity of a philosophical system. However finely spun it may be, the conceptual net cannot contain all the rich, abundant, but often elusive content of human experience. The division of knowledge into distinct subjects, though of obvious practical use as a way of organizing thought about man and the world, is an artificial process which must ultimately be sub-ordinated to a consideration of experience as a whole. Philosophy has no value in itself, but only as systematic reflection upon different aspects of human nature and its relationship with the world; it must always be guided by and subordinated to the reality it seeks to under-stand.

Yet the very fact that any sound philosophical inquiry must begin, in Rousseau's view, with a personal decision to love the truth as well as to seek it, reveals the serious difficulty confronting the modern thinker: the corruption of reason through the influence of the still wider corruption of civilization as a whole makes it extremely diffi-cult to distinguish truth from falsehood, the authentic and original from the merely artificial and accidental features of human existence. Since all values—moral, spiritual, and intellectual—have been per-verted by the social process, the authentic thinker has no starting-point outside himself. At the same time, he has little hope of com-municating his ideas to people who are incapable of understanding them. Before attempting to proclaim the truth, he has to expose the source of error and to make his contemporaries aware of the full extent of their corruption. That is why Rousseau himself divides his work into two parts—the early critical writings which seek to call attention to the evils of modern life, and the later constructive writings which propose an effective remedy.

In his early writings, he is more concerned with destroying the illusory prestige which gives us a stupid admiration for the instruments of our misfortune and with correcting this deceptive evaluation which makes us honour pernicious talents and despise useful values. Everywhere he makes us see the human race better, wiser and happier in its primitive constitu-tion, blind, wretched and wicked as it goes further away from it. His aim is to correct the error of our judgements in order to slow down the pro-gress of our vices and to show us that where we find glory and brilliance, we find in fact only error and misery. (i. 934–5)

Nevertheless, mere critical rejection of the present is not enough; nor is it possible to return to the happiness of the past. 'Human nature does not regress and one can never go back to the times of innocence and equality when one has once left them.' (i. 935.) Thus the critical account of contemporary evils has to be followed by some constructive suggestions for remedying them; it is necessary not only to slow down the rate of corruption, but, if possible, to show the way to happiness, at least to those people and nations—and there may not be many— who are still capable of perceiving and following the truth.

Notes

1. All references, indicated by volume and page number only, are to the *Oeuvres complètes de Jean-Jacques Rousseau*, edited by Bernard Gagnebin and Marcel Raymond, Bibliothèque de la Pléiade, vols. i–iv (Paris, 1959–70). Separate references are given for works not yet included in this edition. All translations are mine.

2. *Correspondance générale de Jean-Jacques Rousseau*, ed. T. Dufour and P.-P. Plan, 20 vols. (Paris, 1924–34), ix. 140.

3. Cf. for example, Robert Derathé's *Le Rationalisme de Jean-Jacques Rousseau* (Paris, 1948), which contains a very enlightening discussion of the role of reason in Rousseau's work.

2
The Criticism of Society

CONSIDERED either as a logical argument or a historical demonstration, Rousseau's *Discours sur les sciences et les arts* is not particularly impressive. That there is a necessary connection between the corruption of man's moral life and the development of culture and that the ancient republics of Greece and Rome were morally superior to large modern states may or may not be true, but it would certainly take more than Rousseau's largely rhetorical exercise to settle the issue. Yet the significance of the *Discours* does not lie in what it seeks to prove but in what it actually says about the position of man in contemporary society; the manner of Rousseau's demonstration is far less important than his intuitive perception of a deep-seated malady which was hidden from most of his contemporaries and to which he himself was made sensitive by his particular personality and position as an 'outsider' living in an alien environment.

⌐The first two *Discours*, as well as the *Lettre à d'Alembert*, contain a searching analysis and indictment of the way in which human nature has become corrupted by the influence of civilization.⌐In the first place, Rousseau insists that the reversal of natural values in society has led to the replacement of 'reality' by 'appearance'. External circumstances no longer correspond to what people really are; outward forms and habits do not express the 'dispositions of the heart';

on the contrary, what men say and do often represents the exact opposite of what they feel. 'Man no longer dares to appear what he is' (ii. 250; iii. 8). 'What he is is nothing, what he appears is everything for him,' says Rousseau of modern man.

As soon as I was in a position to observe men [he told the Archbishop of Paris] I watched them acting and I listened to them talking; then, seeing that their actions did not resemble their speeches, I sought the reason for this dissimilarity, and I found that, since being and appearing were for them two things as different as acting and speaking, this second difference was the cause of the other, and had itself a cause which it remained for me to seek. (iv. 966)

Appearance does not reveal what man is, but serves to conceal his original nature. The social process reinforces the contradiction between appearance and reality by making it impossible for us to know man's true being. Rousseau stresses the point by using the image of the mask. 'The man of society is completely in his mask' (iv. 515). Moreover, the situation is complicated by the further fact that what lies concealed behind the mask is not authentic human nature, but the being who has been corrupted and disfigured by social development. In the preface to the *Discours sur l'inégalité* Rousseau compares modern man to 'the statue of Glaucus which time, sea, and storms have so disfigured that it is less like a god than a wild beast'; the human soul has undergone such a profound transformation that it is now barely recognizable.[1] In the *Dialogues* Rousseau was to combine these ideas of concealment and disfigurement in the image of rust: he described himself as a writer whose first task had been to remove the rust which both hid and corroded man's true features.

The general effect of this concealment and distortion of human nature is to deprive people of individuality, leaving them with no true existence of their own and reducing them to the status of mere puppets. Their personality is sacrificed to the rigid uniformity of social conventions; everybody has to think and act like the rest and can never be truly himself. Man has thus become alienated from his own being and has acquired an artificial self. This loss of personal reality means that 'never being in himself, man is always a stranger to himself and ill at ease when he is compelled to withdraw into himself'. Unlike the self-sufficient primitive man who lives in himself, modern man lives outside himself, basing his life on 'opinion' rather than 'nature', that is, on what others expect him to be rather than on what he really is.

This world of appearances is also misleading because the mask of uniformity merely disguises real feelings. Apparent benevolence hides ruthless self-interest; far from indicating consideration for others, this show of polite benevolence is but a means of concealing men's 'base inclination to do themselves mutual harm'. The perspicacious observer will not be deceived: observing that in society men 'reveal their words and conceal their actions', he will conclude: 'the more they disguise themselves, the more one knows them' (iv. 526). To know men's true character an outsider would simply have to assume that they are the exact opposite of what they seem. Although the masks are constantly changing and men don and doff them 'as do lackeys their livery', they still serve the same selfish purpose. Rousseau accepts as a valid portrait of modern society Hobbes's description of men as mutual enemies; if he criticizes his predecessor, it is mainly for having attributed to natural men characteristics derived from social life.

This 'base and deceptive uniformity' which causes all men to be cast in the same mould, and 'this uniform and perfidious veil', though hiding a jungle-like struggle for existence, are a sign of weakness, not of strength, for they betray man's inability to be himself. It is the weak man, not the strong one, who gives way to his selfish passions. The contemporary world has lost both physical vitality and 'force and vigour of soul' (iii. 8, 22, 23). Moreover, when the modern situation is compared with that of ancient times, it is apparent that this decline in physical strength is due largely to a loss of moral power. Rousseau calls attention to the example of the modern soldier who is so obviously incapable of bearing the great burdens and hardships of the Roman legionaries, not simply because of his physical inferiority, but because of his lack of patriotic fervour. Unlike the soldiers of today, who fight for money alone, Roman soldiers were not mercenaries or professional soldiers, but citizens who, when necessary, gave their lives for freedom and their native land.

Whereas the strength of the ancients lay in their ability to identify themselves with the spirit of their community, modern man has no true 'genius' or original character; he has been taken away from his true self by his subservience to artificial needs and has thus allowed himself to be enslaved by external forces. The moral power of ancient communities provided their members with a source of inner strength and unity; civilized life, on the other hand, is marked by the contraction of personal existence and the tendency of people to develop one side of their character and to satisfy one particular appetite at the expense of the rest. This hypertrophy of personality is clearly revealed in the feverish pursuit of material possessions which, far from being treated as a means of survival, have become an end in themselves. In the same way, knowledge, divorced from its human context, has degenerated into 'vain science' and 'futile curiosity'; instead of being seekers of truth, thinkers have become nothing but 'proud reasoners'. Language too has ceased to be a valid means of communication and is merely the instrument of false taste or empty social jargon, comparable in many ways to the other inessential 'accoutrements' of modern life (iii. 9–14).

This loss of personal strength has led inevitably to the enslavement of modern man. Because the 'study of the sciences softens courage and makes it effeminate', man has become the victim of his own weakness (iii. 168, 222); reflection has had a debilitating effect upon his character. As Rousseau affirms in the *Contrat social*, it is ironical that the very society which claims to be superior to the ancients because it does not possess slaves, should allow itself to be subjected to more subtle and insidious forms of dependence. 'Civil man lives and dies in enslavement' (iv. 253). This is the theme to which Rousseau constantly returns. Whatever the original purpose of his existence, modern man is certainly 'in chains'; his lack of moral strength has made him dependent on external things, so that even those needs which he considers to be necessary to his existence are nothing but the artificial products of his corrupt environment. The distortion and weakening of personal life are the inevitable consequence of man's foolish striving for false goals.

Rousseau is thus one of the first modern thinkers to have insisted upon the idea of man's alienation from his original being. 'We no

longer exist where we are,' he affirms in *Émile*, 'we exist only where
we are not' (iv. 308). Having become a stranger to himself, man soon
forgets his own being; he has lost all sense of possessing a personal
centre capable of conferring unity and order on his existence. Rousseau insists that one of the main reasons for this estrangement is the
disastrous influence of urban life, which makes people other than
what they ought to be and invests them with a new but artificial
being. As Saint-Preux well puts it: 'It is the first inconvenience of
large towns that in them men become other than what they are, and
that society gives them so to speak a being different from their own'
(ii. 273). Towns are the 'abyss of the human race':

Men are not meant to be heaped up in ant-hills but to be scattered over the
earth they cultivate. The more they gather together, the more they corrupt one another. The infirmities of the body as well as the vices of the
soul are the inevitable effect of this excessive concourse. Of all the animals
man is the one who can least live in herds. Men heaped together like sheep
would all soon perish. Man's breath is fatal to his fellows: this is not less
true literally than figuratively. (iv. 276–7)

Rousseau points out that this process of alienation has not brought
peace, but only a state of acute inner conflict. Although man has
become other than his true self, he has not found personal unity, for
he is constantly at war with himself; restless and tormented, he seeks
happiness through activities which never bring him fulfilment. Unlike his primitive ancestors who lived peaceful, harmonious lives, he
is always 'in contradiction with himself'.

This condition of inner contradiction is clearly revealed in his
persistent anxiety. The man who lives outside himself is a prey to
insecurity; as he vainly seeks to achieve an aim which is incompatible
with his real nature, he can never find genuine contentment, but is
constantly subjected to restlessness and uncertainty. Rousseau points
out that the multifarious activities and intrigues of the modern world,
being inspired by an insatiable appetite for personal gain, merely
betray man's inability to know his true nature. 'The anxious, restless
spirit of this age' is reflected in modern man's attitude towards time:
an anxious being cannot live in a single temporal dimension; although
he fears the present without having confidence in the future, he still

looks to the future to overcome his dissatisfaction with the present; he is preoccupied by a 'foresight' which 'casts him beyond himself' and makes him hold the present to be of no account (iv. 302, 307). On other occasions he escapes from the present by yearning for the irrecoverable past, or falling into a mood of stultifying *ennui*.

Rousseau sees a typical product of modern decadence in the theatre. It is not necessary to reproduce here his detailed indictment of the theatre, but it may be helpful to relate his main observations on the subject to his general criticism of contemporary society. His argument is based on the assumption that a man's real pleasures 'derive from his nature and spring from his labours, relationships, and needs'. The theatre, on the other hand, is an essentially artificial form of entertainment brought into being by the corrupt passions and emotions of modern society; it reflects the general deterioration of human values, for it is always the servant of contemporary needs, never their master. Our need 'to put our heart on the stage as though it were ill at ease within us' shows how an essential part of ourselves has become detached from the rest of our personality and transformed into a public spectacle. By contemplating this artificial object each one isolates himself from the rest, and shuts himself up within his own consciousness in order to enjoy the sight of something that has no living relationship with his inner life. In the theatre we 'forget ourselves and become concerned with external objects'. Nothing presented on the stage can be close to us and, as Rousseau is at pains to emphasize, by that very fact any emotions aroused by the objects of our contemplation must be sterile and transitory. The theatre is a typical example of an activity that prefers appearance to reality. The actor himself, as a man whose condition is to appear, divests himself of his own personality in order to take on an artificial character; he is an imitator, constantly trying to be other than what he is, making a base traffic of himself, selling his appearances for money; he is not a 'man, the noblest of all beings', but a creature who allows himself to be 'the plaything of the spectators'.[2]

Rousseau lays particular stress upon the form of the theatre: he describes it as a 'dark prison', in which the audience sits silent and motionless, fascinated by the spectacle on the stage before them and thereby transformed into symbols of servitude. Such an existence can only enervate man's moral being and make him incapable of personal decision and action. The theme of imprisonment is again emphasized when Rousseau describes the life of the contemporary *salons*, those 'voluntary prisons' in which men incarcerate themselves in order to become the slaves of 'childish habits'; stifling in 'enclosed rooms', they perform their ritual before a female 'idol', who moves only her tongue and eyes and delights in softening the character of the effeminate beings so eager to pay her this degrading homage. The *salons*, like the theatre, are characteristic of an environment in which people are only too anxious to forget themselves in order to become 'the apes of the large towns'; they do not live in themselves but in others.[3]

The predominance of women in both the theatre (where love is the most popular theme) and the *salons* (where so-called love is again the main preoccupation) is a significant expression of the reversal of natural relationships so characteristic of the modern world. Rousseau always insists that woman's most characteristic attribute is—or ought to be—her modesty or *pudeur*: the true woman is content to identify herself with her home and her family, deliberately refraining from making a public exhibition of herself. In the theatre—as in the *salons* —on the other hand, she seeks a position of dominance, making herself an arbiter of public opinion and even trying to lay down rules of literary taste. Nature, affirms Rousseau, did not make woman inferior to man but simply intended her for a different role; to attempt to give her a masculine role is to rob her of her true character. Both nature and reason require women to lead a quiet retired life with their household and family. Because their typical qualities are docility and gentleness, they must play a subordinate social role and adapt themselves to the idea that they are at the mercy of men's judgements and that their true happiness consists of pleasing men and earning their good opinion (iv. 703). By letting them make a spectacle of themselves on the stage or in the *salons* modern society is thrusting them into behaviour for which they are completely unsuited by nature and temperament.

Although Rousseau insists that this reversal of natural feelings must lead to a grave distortion of human values by setting people in conflict with themselves, he does not seek to resolve the problem in his early writings, but contents himself with giving some brief indications of the positive principles which can help to halt or reverse the disastrous trend. The chief value extolled in the first *Discours* is virtue, the 'sublime science of simple souls', which can be learnt by anyone who 'withdraws into himself and listens to the voice of his conscience in the silence of the passions' (iii. 30). Such, affirms Rousseau, is the only true philosophy worthy of those who wish to do rather than talk. At this stage, he does not analyse the concept of virtue, but its very simplicity suggests that it is a powerful unifying force which gives man the moral strength to resist the corruption of his time. Instead of seeking material wealth and luxury, the virtuous man will rely on the simple frugality required by his inner strength.

Rousseau praises the ancient republics of Greece and Rome as examples of this heroic morality. In particular, he singles out Sparta rather than Athens for special praise. Whereas Athens was the centre of culture and ultimately became weakened by its love of knowledge, Sparta preferred to cultivate civic virtues and made itself into a nation of demigods. Of the heroes of Antiquity, Cato is an outstanding example—'the greatest of men'—remarkable for his moral courage and firmness, attacking 'the deceitful and subtle Greeks who were seducing the virtue and weakening the courage of his fellow citizens' (iii. 14); he steadfastly refused to 'sully his great soul' with the crimes of his contemporaries. Brutus too—the father who let his sons be condemned to death rather than betray the Republic—is another example of remarkable civic virtue. In all this Rousseau is not unmindful of his enthusiasm for Plutarch, one of his favourite childhood authors and a life-long literary love. Men such as these gave humanity 'the sight and model of the purest virtue that ever existed' and 'taught men to resist the evils of their age and detest the horrible maxim of society people that we must do like the rest' (iii. 87).

The necessity of virtue is based largely on the need to combat the corruption of the age. Rousseau finds it significant that Cato was acutely conscious of the dangers threatening the Roman Republic. Virtue thus suggests a certain rigidity, a sort of heroic defiance of worldly values. In more propitious circumstances, when man is less exposed to such harmful influences and when he feels himself free to indulge in more spontaneous emotions, there is not the same need for austere virtue. No doubt it is no longer possible to recognize the simplicity of early times. 'It is a fine shore, adorned by nature's hands alone, towards which we constantly turn our gaze, and which we regretfully feel to be moving away from us' (iii. 22). Although this yearning for past happiness can never be made the basis of practical life, Rousseau believes that man can do much to protect himself against the harmful effects of modern civilization by abandoning the towns for the countryside. In this way he not only escapes from the stifling effects of city-life and has more space in which to move and breathe, but he is also in closer contact with the resources of physical nature. The Ancients wisely tried to let all their entertainments take place against the background of nature and, at the same time, based them on a genuine sense of communal and social unity. The Greek theatre is an excellent example of this attitude. Instead of being an isolated and artificial form of entertainment herding people together in a darkened building, as is the case today, the performances of the Greek theatre took place out of doors and drew their subject-matter and inspiration from the history of the community. Like the Ancients, the modern Genevans, who still love the country and the open air, are provided with a suitable setting for the enjoyment of 'simple, innocent activities' appropriate to 'republican manners'; they must have pleasures which are worthy of a 'free people' and still reminiscent of that 'ancient ruggedness which preserves a good constitution as well as good habits'. 'These touching and tender sights' will be inspired, like those of the Greeks, by themes taken from the history of the Republic; both pleasures and duties will be drawn from the people's own past, not from some alien source. Equally appropriate would be public festivals which do not take place in some 'dark cavern' but in the open air. 'It is in the open air, beneath the sky, that you must gather and abandon yourselves to the sweet feeling of your happiness.'[4]

Such entertainment has the great merit of allowing people to become open to one another. 'Make each one love and see himself in the others, so that all may be the better united.'[5] The happiness of former ages lay in men's remarkable capacity for being able to 'penetrate one another reciprocally' (iii. 8). In the *Dédicace* to the second *Discours* Rousseau again reminds the Genevans that they have not lost 'this sweet habit of seeing and knowing one another'. 'The only pure joy is public joy and nature's true feelings hold sway only over the people.'[6] Experiences such as these allow men to establish close contact with physical nature and with one another. The unity of existence is thereby restored in a way that brings men back to the 'peace, freedom, equity and innocence' which are the prerequisites of 'solid happiness'.

Notes

1. iii. 122. Cf. J. Starobinski, *Jean-Jacques Rousseau, la transparence et l'obstacle* (2nd ed., Paris, 1971), p. 28.

2. Cf. *Lettre à d'Alembert sur les spectacles*, ed. M. Fuchs (Geneva, 1948), pp. 24, 90, and *passim*.

3. Ibid., pp. 92, 103.

4. Ibid., pp. 168, 184.

5. Ibid., p. 169.

6. Ibid., p. 182 n.

3
The State of Nature and the Nature of Man

In spite of the strongly critical emphasis of the first *Discours*, Rousseau's thought is already dominated by a fundamental antithesis—the antithesis between the 'original' nature of man and the corruption of modern society; in the same way the freedom of man's true being is contrasted with his present enslavement. The antithetical form of Rousseau's argument is further reinforced by his determination to confront contemporary decadence with the noble virtue of ancient republics and their heroes as well as with the less clearly defined 'nature' which man has allegedly abandoned with such dire consequences. Although the terms 'nature' and 'natural' obviously play an important part in Rousseau's thought as a whole, their main function in his early work is to serve as critical principles determining the gravity of man's immediate situation; nature is what man is *not* rather than what he ought to be; as such, it remains at first a somewhat indefinite concept, even though it possesses fundamental significance as a means of making men aware of the full extent of their corruption. Here, as elsewhere in Rousseau's work, a basic concept has first of all to be defined in terms of its opposite.

Rousseau considers the notion of man's original nature to be inseparable from an analysis of the processes which have been responsible for its perversion; it is impossible to delineate the authentic

features of man's existence without first of all indicating the main
stages of its descent into misery and corruption. Nevertheless, Rousseau makes it clear at the very beginning of his *Discours sur l'inégalité*
that he is not concerned with history in any scientific sense. This follows quite logically from his philosophical method which relies more
on intuitively perceived principles than on empirical observation. His
reconstruction of human history is purely hypothetical, its purpose
being to throw light on man's original nature rather than on the
actual circumstances of his development; he is not concerned with
facts as such, but with a need to distinguish between the original
and artificial elements of man's being. This is the central theme of
Rousseau's work and explains his refusal to let his thought be restricted by the methodology of any specific science. To arrive at the
truth about human nature it is necessary, in his view, to go beyond
the limitations of particular intellectual disciplines and examine the
fundamental features of human existence, for these will necessarily
determine the thinker's attitude towards the various branches of
knowledge. In his later works Rousseau was to stress this wider aspect
when he described himself as 'the painter and apologist of nature' as
well as 'the historian of the human heart' (i. 936).

In spite of his desire to establish first principles, Rousseau could
not completely avoid the ambiguity implicit in the idea of man's
original being. Although human nature involves more than the results of a historical process, it cannot be completely separated from
the idea of its development in time. The 'painter and portrayer' of
basic principles is also the 'historian' of psychological development. In
the deepest sense, 'original' means what is essential and authentic, or
in Rousseau's words, 'what belongs incontestably to man' as opposed
to what is accidental and artificial. It is difficult, however, to attribute
any precise meaning to these notions without some consideration of
man's historical development; in order to understand his fundamental nature, it is necessary to go back to his temporal origins; even
though these origins do not reveal his complete being, they express
the purity and simplicity of primordial feelings which have not been
corrupted by society. The idea of 'the state of nature' is thus a mere
starting-point for the consideration of a larger problem. Rousseau
admits that he is describing 'a state which exists no longer, which

perhaps has never existed, which probably will never exist', but which can provide a means of 'judging our present condition' by 'disentangling what is original and artificial in man's present nature' (iii. 123). Rousseau attributes earlier philosophical confusion to erroneous views about the nature of man and its relationship with natural law. To solve this problem it is necessary to abandon scientific treatises and reflect upon the 'first and simplest operations of the human soul', as Rousseau himself had done when he first meditated his *Discours sur l'inégalité* in the forest of Saint-Germain, where he sought 'the image of those early times of which he proudly traced the history', 'making a clean sweep of men's petty lies', revealing to them the meaning of nature and 'comparing man's man to natural man' (i. 388). Although any account of human history is bound to be conjectural, this is unimportant, since it is not a question of advancing 'historical truths', but only 'hypothetical and conditional reasonings' intended to 'illuminate the nature of things' rather than to 'show their true origin' (iii. 133). No doubt the notes appended to the second *Discours* put forward scientific and historical evidence drawn from travel-books as well as from scientific and philosophical treatises such as those of Locke, Buffon, and Condillac, but this supporting testimony is meant simply to confirm the conjectures made on intuitive grounds.

'Nature' and the 'nature of man' are, then, much more fundamental concepts than the 'state of nature' and the pseudo-historical account of man's evolution from primitive conditions to his existence in the modern world, since they provide normative and critical principles for distinguishing between the original and the inessential aspects of man's being. 'Nature' cannot have a merely historical meaning, because history represents little more than the decline and fall of human existence from innocence into enslavement and corruption; the historical process can be judged only by a principle which transcends it and yet gives it meaning. Although nature is thus a critical principle which enables us to see how present existence is at variance with human nature in its deepest sense, it also represents an ontological and metaphysical principle of more positive significance, for human nature cannot be properly understood unless it is related to a still more fundamental reality, of which it is intended to be an integral part. The difficulties involved in the concept of nature, as we shall see, are bound up with the fact that this fundamental nature already exists as the ordered system of the universe created by God, even though it may not be clearly perceived by men who have been corrupted by the social process; 'nature' undoubtedly exists, but it is not adequately known. Moreover, man's present condition suggests that human nature, in the original sense of the term, is as yet only potential; man will have fulfilled himself only when he has properly developed the authentic possibilities of his being. On the other hand, these possibilities cannot be realized until he has perceived their relationship with the universal order. 'Nature' thus has a broad metaphysical significance as the universal order, and a more limited and less clearly defined meaning as human nature in its potential perfection.

The concept of the 'state of nature' is obviously much less fundamental than the metaphysical nature of the universal order or the ideal nature of the fulfilled human being, but it can be related to nature in a third and still more limited sense as the primordial biological and affective impulses animating man in the very early stages of his existence. The state of nature constitutes a rudimentary phase of human existence and yet, in a temporal sense, it is an original form of being in as much as it has not yet been spoilt by the influence of society. Although all genuine trace of this original state of nature has been lost, Rousseau believes it reasonable to suppose that man has passed through a pre-social phase of development. After making some intelligent conjectures about this condition, we may find, he affirms, limited supporting evidence for them in an examination of peoples who have not yet been corrupted by European society.

This idea of the state of nature was familiar to many thinkers before Rousseau, and especially to those of the Natural Law School such as Grotius and Pufendorf. Although some predecessors had accorded it a historical status, by Rousseau's time its hypothetical function had been widely admitted, and, as Rousseau's preface makes clear, its main purpose was to throw light on the nature of man before he entered social life. More important, therefore, than the historical role of the concept were its implications for the understanding of the human condition. Although Rousseau was by no means the first thinker to ignore the historical aspect, he differed from his predecessors in one important respect: while they had treated human existence in a fairly static way, endowing primitive man with many essential characteristics of social man, he stressed the idea of man as a being who acquired new powers and capacities in the course of his development. Whereas Grotius and Pufendorf, for example, had considered primitive man as essentially rational and social—a view accepted by a later thinker like Locke—Rousseau treated the state of nature as a mere starting-point, as the stage at which man possessed the minimal qualities which distinguished him from the animals; in his opinion, primitive man was a purely instinctive creature devoid of intellectual and moral attributes. Although Hobbes had already held a similar view, he had also insisted that man's basically aggressive, self-seeking nature was not radically altered by society, but was merely held in check by the force of the laws; men were made moral by the constraints to which they were subjected—for their own good —as soon as they entered the civil association. Rousseau, on the other hand, believed in man's capacity for development and possible improvement. Of these earlier thinkers only Spinoza seems to have given society a similar role in developing rationality and freedom in a being hitherto dominated by feeling and instinct.

At this early stage of human existence, therefore, 'nature' means little more than basic physical and psychological impulses or, in Rousseau's words, the 'primitive disposition' necessary for survival. Since savage man has no moral or intellectual needs, he is a creature of instinct, physically strong and adaptable and endowed with a sensibility that allows him to exist in harmony with his environment. Although Rousseau agrees with Hobbes in denying primitive man the moral sense and sociability attributed to him by the Natural Law School, he emphatically denies that man is 'naturally wicked' or 'vicious'. On the contrary, the state of nature is a peaceful one, allowing men to lead an isolated, independent existence that involves them in no serious conflict with one another. Primitive man is dominated by two fundamental urges: the first is the basic impulse of self-preservation, which is easily satisfied in a physical environment favourable to survival; at the same time he is prevented from being wantonly aggressive towards others by the impulse of 'natural pity', which is a spontaneous aversion to the sight of suffering.

While never suggesting that such a mode of existence could be acceptable to the mature human being (the absence of ethical criteria would in any case make any serious comparison between primitive and social man impossible), Rousseau believes that the state of nature had one great advantage over man's present condition: it allowed him to enjoy a happiness completely unknown to later generations. The principal reason for this was primitive man's ability to identify himself effortlessly with his own true nature and to be content with his immediate being; he was able to live in himself, whereas modern man has constantly to be outside himself. A creature of instinct, he was at peace with himself because he was faithful to his own nature. 'His soul, which nothing disturbs, abandons itself to the sole feeling of its present existence, without any idea of the future, however close it may be' (iii. 144). He is happy because he is without 'foresight or curiosity'. His existence is characterized by a fundamental unity which makes him largely self-sufficient, for he is 'always ready to bear himself, so to speak, entirely with himself'. Instinct allows the un-inhibited and peaceful satisfaction of his desires and the enjoyment of his immediate existence.

Modern man, on the other hand, is governed by artificial needs which can be satisfied only with the help of other people. His position is thus one of dependence. His misery is also aggravated by another evil: not only is he dependent upon others, but he has also become the victim of his own misguided efforts to find contentment. This process was initiated by 'his first look at himself', which not only made him aware of himself as a separate being, but also aware of others as different from himself. For the first time, he became the object of his own consciousness as well as of other people's. 'Each began to look at others and wanted to be looked at himself' (iii. 169).

Man's dependence on others soon had serious psychological, as well as physical, repercussions upon his whole way of life. Whereas the static untroubled condition of primitive man had allowed him to be 'healthy, good, and happy' in his 'simple, uniform, and lonely way of life', modern man has been made 'weak, fearful, and cringing' by his 'softened, effeminate mode of life' (iii. 137–9). No longer willing or able to accept the simple existence of his forebears, he has become a tormented, inwardly divided being looking anxiously outside himself. Characteristic adult faculties such as imagination and reflection have served only to increase his inner disquiet by taking him further and further away from his natural condition and making him aware of himself as a separate but divided being.

As we shall see, Rousseau does not believe that this movement towards misery need be inevitable, but he insists that it has created one of the gravest problems of modern life—inequality. The physical inequality which existed in the state of nature did not constitute a problem; being in direct contact with their physical environment, rather than with one another, primitive men were able to satisfy their needs by their own efforts. In the state of nature there was 'a real and indestructible equality, because physical differences between individuals were not important and certainly not great enough to make one man dependent on another' (iv. 524). Moreover, this equality was governed by men's relations with things rather than with one another; the situation was the same for all and no one was favoured at the expense of the rest. In society, on the other hand, people are forced to compete with one another, so that the weak are at the mercy of the strong and the inequality which was insignificant in the state of nature assumes overriding importance and has permanent effects; it is no longer a question of a physical inequality associated with the 'harsh yoke of necessity', but of a 'conventional' or artificial inequality depending upon the human will and resulting from men's close but conflicting relations with one another. Instead of all being subjected to a single form of physical necessity and dependence, they are split into two groups: strong and weak, masters and slaves.

The main purpose of the second part of the *Discours sur l'inégalité* is to show how this inequality came about. Rousseau points out that men did not suddenly move forward from the state of nature to civil life; political society was the result of a long historical process. No doubt some unexpected physical phenomenon was responsible for the initial movement away from nature, for Rousseau does not believe that men would willingly have abandoned a condition which brought them so much peace and happiness. On the other hand, although an external cause was necessary to bring about the change, this would have been insufficient without the help of certain innate potentialities embryonically present in man from the very first; it was these potentialities which enabled him to go beyond his primitive condition. In its most rudimentary form nature represents a static, circumscribed world in which all creatures live according to basic physical laws and follow the same unvarying patterns of behaviour. At this level, it is difficult at first sight to distinguish between animals and humans, because both are animated by physical appetite and sensibility, and dominated by the demands of pleasure and pain; since there is very little room for development or sudden change, the natural being, whether man or animal, soon reaches maturity and thereafter follows the same unvarying pattern of behaviour. However, even at this primitive stage, there already exists an important difference between men and animals: although primitive man is apparently little more than a creature of instinct, devoid of morality and reflection, he possesses certain 'virtual' capacities, unknown to the animal kingdom. In the state of nature itself, he is more adaptable than the animals, often being able to overcome creatures physically stronger than himself. This is because 'nature commands every animal and the beast obeys', while 'man experiences the same impression, but recognizes that he is free to acquiesce or resist'; it is his 'power to will or rather to choose'—'the consciousness of his freedom'—that reveals his ability to escape from subjection to 'mechanical' forces and exert himself as a 'free agent' (iii. 141). No doubt this capacity is dormant in the state of nature, but man's freedom will express itself actively in suitable conditions.

Moreover, man has a second and equally important characteristic which distinguishes him from the animals: whereas the animal attains full growth at the end of a comparatively short period of time and thereafter does not change, man has the power to perfect himself and move on to new and more complex modes of being. Rousseau lays great stress on this idea of man's perfectibility which plays an important role in his whole philosophy of human nature. He admits that perfectibility can be a source of misery as well as happiness, for if man can rise higher than the animals, he can also become more degraded than they: perfectibility presupposes the possibility of decline as well as improvement, but, whatever its consequences, it is an ineradicable feature of human nature; man has continually to move forward to a new stage of development, as 'his primitive dispositions are extended and strengthened' (iv. 248).

In view of all this, it is not surprising to find primitive man leaving the state of nature as soon as physical circumstances favour the development of his dormant capacities. At the same time Rousseau recognizes that this new situation has several puzzling features. The emergence of language, for example—one of man's most characteristic attributes—seems an inexplicable phenomenon, since it cannot exist without society which, in its turn, cannot exist without language; it is difficult to explain the appearance of language or society among isolated beings who have no need of either. Rousseau accepts Condillac's point that language presupposes reflection and imagination (faculties unknown to primitive man), but he insists that their development is impossible without the existence of social relations. Whatever may be the truth about the origin of language, Rousseau affirms that men's increasingly close relations with one another eventually led to the formation of rudimentary moral attitudes and to a willingness to base conduct on agreed principles. Whereas the solitude of the state of nature had involved no kind of moral relation or obligation and produced neither vices nor virtues, the developing human being began to perceive 'certain relations', to indulge in 'some kind of reflection', and to show 'a mechanical prudence which indicated the precautions most necessary to his safety'. A decisive stage in human history was reached with the 'establishment and distinction of families' and the introduction of 'a kind of property' (iii. 164–7). The appearance of this simple society constituted the first social revolution—an event that was important not simply because it brought men together for the first time, but also because of its effects upon their nature; it changed both their mental and emotional outlook as they became aware of themselves and other people.

Unfortunately this change of attitude already foreshadowed some of the later evils of civilized life—for example, the pride and vanity which resulted from the individual's desire to 'look at himself and compare himself with others'; as soon as he began to treat himself as a separate being, he inevitably began to see himself as the rival of other people. At first these drawbacks were easily outweighed by considerable benefits: men experienced satisfactions which had been denied to their ancestors. In particular they enjoyed 'the sweetest feelings known to men, conjugal and paternal love' (iii. 168). Moreover, all family attachments were both reciprocal and free. Life was still simple and solitary with very limited needs and adequate means of satisfying them. Yet the use of hitherto unknown 'commodities' already constituted a potential threat to future happiness by 'softening both body and mind'. Especially insidious in its effects was the feeling of deprivation experienced by those who foolishly resented their inability to obtain superfluous commodities; they were 'unhappy to lose them without being happy to possess them' (iii. 168). More important, therefore, than the lack of material goods were the psychological effects of possession and deprivation which began to react upon men's relations with one another. The mere goodness of their earlier state and the spontaneous expression of innate feelings gave way to moral reactions associated with pride and envy. Nevertheless, these disadvantages and difficulties were not grave enough to upset the balance of human existence and, all things considered, this was probably the happiest period of man's existence: 'being placed by nature half-way between the stupidity of the brutes and the fatal enlightenment of civil man and limited equally by instinct and reason to protecting himself from the evil which threatens him, he is restrained by natural pity from doing harm to anyone, and is not impelled to it, even after receiving harm' (iii. 170). Unlike primitive man, this first social man uses his reason, and yet in a way that harmonizes with his simple needs. This phase of human development, concludes Rousseau, keeping 'a just balance between the indolence of the primitive state and the lively activity of our pride, must have been the happiest and most durable period' in human history (iii. 171). There were no violent changes and men enjoyed a sense of security and stability; since they were not dependent on others, they were still versatile enough to make their own tools and be largely self-sufficient. They could be 'free, healthy, good and happy' and yet enjoy the pleasures of 'independent intercourse'.

It is not necessary to give a detailed account of Rousseau's reconstruction of human history which, he affirms, resulted in the 'perfection of the individual' and the 'deterioration of the species', for, as man began to develop individual capacities advantageous to himself, it became increasingly difficult for him to live with his fellow-men. There then occurred a second social revolution which completely altered the course of human existence. The discovery of metallurgy and agriculture led to the division of labour and the establishment of property, with a disastrous distinction between 'mine' and 'thine' that was to put men in permanent conflict with one another. The most significant consequence of this change was the emergence of inequality as an inescapable feature of the human situation. At the same time these new conditions led to a rapid development of human faculties—memory, imagination, reason, and pride—all of which made life more difficult and complex. One of the most striking features of modern society now revealed itself for the first time: 'it was necessary for people to show themselves other than what they in fact were. Being and appearing became two different things, and from this distinction emerged the imposing ostentation, the deceitful cunning and all the vices which follow in their train' (iii. 174). Because of the disastrous effects of inequality, freedom was replaced by servitude. Even the rich were enslaved by the poor, because rich and poor could not exist without each other.

The inequality created by property produced anxiety, insecurity, and conflict, as each man struggled to become as rich and as powerful as possible and to put himself above others. People were no longer content to satisfy their needs; they went on to seek, first, abundance, and then superfluity. All became inspired with the 'dark inclination to do themselves mutual harm'. At this point Rousseau recalls the theme of the first *Discours* with its stress on concealment: men hid behind their masks in order to satisfy 'their hidden desire to achieve their own profit at others' expense'. They soon lived in the state of mutual enmity attributed by Hobbes to man in the state of nature. Rousseau, however, ascribes this war of all against all to the defects of the social state, not to man's original being. The desire for material possessions determined all men's actions, and the rich were like 'hungry wolves who, having once tasted human flesh, will be satisfied with no other food'. In this way, men became 'greedy, ambitious and wicked'. The harmonious relationships of the early societies now gave way to 'the most horrible state of war' (iii. 175–6).

Rousseau lays particular stress on the role of the rich in the resolution of this problem of constant strife. They were the people who were likely to lose most in the perpetual war, for any right they could claim for their usurpations was obviously precarious and deceptive; they always ran the risk of being dispossessed by the very force which had enabled them to accumulate their wealth. To end this state of insecurity they finally devised 'the most carefully conceived plan that ever entered the human mind'; they suggested the establishment of a supreme power which would govern men according to the laws and which would 'defend and protect all the members of the association, repulse common enemies, and maintain them in eternal concord' (iii. 177). The founding of an association governed by law would thereby transform a merely natural right based on force into a legal right supported by universal consent. According to Rousseau, this was how political society came into being. In fact, this agreement or contract was a gigantic confidence-trick perpetuated by the rich at the expense of the poor, who gained nothing from it except permanent enslavement. The rich were able to achieve this end, because it was not difficult for ruthless, astute men to persuade their simple, untutored fellows that the new society would be to their benefit; the poor mistakenly believed that they were deriving real security from this changed situation. 'All hastened to put on their chains in the belief that they were assuring their freedom.' Property and inequality were henceforth sanctioned by law, so that natural freedom was for ever destroyed. 'For the profit of a few ambitious men' the whole human race was subjected to 'toil, servitude, and misery' (iii. 176–8).

The establishment of one political society soon led to others and civil right quickly became a general feature of human existence as citizens acknowledged the need for a common rule. Henceforth, the state of nature existed only between nations in so far as they acknowledged no authority higher than their own strength and power; the only concession to law was the recognition of *le droit des gens*, or 'tacit conventions', which, though not legally binding, were accepted as the practical basis of international relations.

The formation of political society thus constituted a decisive, if disastrous, phase in human history, all the more deplorable because it appeared to rest on conventions intended for the benefit of all. In fact, however, the strong oppressed the weak under the cover of the law. Already in the second *Discours* Rousseau puts forward his favourite idea that political power always works to the advantage of the strong and the detriment of the weak—an idea that has been warmly approved by Marxist commentators. (His insistence on the corrupting influence of power, as we shall see, explains the strain of pessimism running through his political writings.) Before the establishment of property it is perhaps more appropriate to speak of the distinction between rich and poor; after the institution of legal government, it was a question of powerful and weak, since man's position in society was henceforth determined by the laws. At first these laws were probably crude and ineffective, consisting of little more than a few general conventions, but the awareness of many inconveniences and disorders gradually led to various modifications, and, in particular, to the entrusting of public authority (a dangerous innovation) to particular individuals or 'magistrates'. Yet in all this Rousseau insists upon a point that is to become of cardinal importance in the political theory of the *Contrat social*: however unjust a political society may be, its original purpose is to secure the freedom of its members and the protection of their lives and property. Rousseau holds fast to the idea of the contractual basis of society: however gullible and foolish they may be, men always appoint leaders to defend their freedom, not to destroy it. This goal is never attained, because the civil association serves merely to stabilize existing inequalities and prevent the exercise of true freedom. Moreover, power itself has a pernicious influence upon those who exercise it, and magistrates soon try to transform their office into a hereditary right. Instead of a society of free men, there eventually exists only a society of slaves; the leaders are replaced by a single ruler who governs by his own power alone, reducing all citizens to a state of subjection. Such, according to Rousseau, are the three main phases in the development of inequality: rich and poor, powerful and weak, master and slaves. The final stage appears when the 'monster' of despotism rears 'its hideous head' (iii. 190); with the advent of despotism the historical process has come full circle, since it has produced a new but corrupt 'state of nature' based on force alone. The historical process which began with the freedom and independence of the state of nature thus ends with the suppression of the very characteristic which is supposed to make men truly human; instead of being free, they have been transformed into abject slaves.

4

The Psychological Development
of the Individual

SINCE man's history is, for the most part, one of gradual enslavement and degradation, Rousseau does not believe that an adequate
knowledge of his true nature can be obtained from a mere study of
the past. At most, the reconstruction of man's early history will
reveal the presence of capacities which, after an initial period of happy
and spontaneous development, were disastrously diverted from their
true function. Nevertheless, even the misuse of these innate powers
shows that human nature cannot be identified with its primitive
condition; man is constantly moving forward to new and more complex modes of being; the fact that at one moment in his history he
chose to follow the wrong path in no way affects his essential nature
as a being capable of harmonious development in propitious circumstances. The spectacle of the unhappy past should spur on the thinker
to envisage what man might have become had he made the right
choice. Indeed, Rousseau makes it clear that a detailed analysis of
man's essential being—that is, his authentic, as opposed to his merely
historical, nature—might still offer some hope of slowing down, if
not halting, the process of decline; in particularly favourable conditions it might even be possible to allow a new nature to emerge.
Far from being a merely critical principle for measuring the extent of

man's degradation, 'nature' could become a positive ideal responsible for the discovery of new wisdom and the regeneration of humanity.

After describing man's position in contemporary society and tracing his development from the state of nature to the present time, Rousseau turns to the task of giving a more constructive view of human nature. To distinguish between its original and artificial aspects, he has to go more fully into the question of the human condition. He abandons the hypothetical and pseudo-historical reconstruction of the 'state of nature' in order to examine the living individual and see what he would become if he were allowed to follow his own innate capacities and the impulse of nature, rather than the dictates of society and opinion. Rousseau realizes that his discussion of the education of the individual must involve normative principles, since he is anticipating what might be rather than anything that actually exists; he has to have some conception of man's ideal possibilities if he is to suggest adequate means of realizing them. At the same time he does not think that his account of human development is merely utopian in the sense of being completely remote from reality, for he is not dealing with chimerical beings, but with the authentic possibilities of 'original' human nature. (In this respect, the mixture of idealistic and realistic elements in *Émile* is rather similar to the treatment of political problems in the *Contrat social*.) Because his guiding principles cannot be derived from an examination of empirical reality, even though they are ultimately conceived as applicable to real people, he acknowledges the importance of obtaining some kind of insight into the essential features of human existence.

Rousseau makes it clear that his main object in *Émile* is not to produce a manual of education, for his 'true study is that of the human condition'. Before it intends him for any particular profession, 'nature calls the child to human life' (iv. 252). Accordingly, Rousseau affirms: 'To live is the profession I wish to teach him.' His primary concern, therefore, is with an analysis of human nature rather than with the merely pragmatic aspects of the child's education, his eventual aim being to describe the development of the complete individual—of man himself—from childhood to maturity.

Rousseau undertakes his task with a certain optimism, because he has confidence in the possibilities of human nature. As he points out in one of his personal works, *Émile* is not a manual of education, but a 'philosophical treatise on man's natural goodness' (i. 934). A survey of the contemporary scene will undoubtedly show that 'men are wicked', but this in no way conflicts with the equally important fact that 'man is naturally good' (iii. 202); human nature in its essence and intrinsic possibilities—as opposed to its historical and accidental characteristics—is good. This means that since evil is not a part of man's original nature, it must have some external source, and Rousseau's intention is 'to show how vice and error, being foreign to man's constitution, are introduced into it from the outside and gradually change it for the worse' (i. 934). The principle of natural goodness is thus combined with the rational explanation of how it has become perverted by human error. 'Let us lay down', says Rousseau, 'as an incontrovertible maxim that nature's first movements are always right: there is no original perversity in the human heart: there is not a single vice in it, of which I cannot say how and where it came in' (iv. 322). The same principle is reiterated in the *Lettre à Beaumont*:

The fundamental principle of all morality ... is that man is a naturally good being loving justice and order; that there is no original perversity in the human heart, and that the first movements of nature are always right ... I have described the way in which they are born and I have followed so to speak their genealogy, and I have shown how, by the gradual deterioration of their original goodness, men become what they are. (iv. 935–6)

One conclusion immediately follows: in order to ensure the harmonious development of the child's original being, it is necessary to remove all corrupting external influences and allow nature to follow its own course. A preliminary condition for achieving this is to remove the child from the evil influence of the towns and bring him up in the country. Rousseau insists on this point at the beginning of *Émile*, and it is in perfect accord with his condemnation of contemporary society. Apart from protecting the child against harmful influences, a rural environment will also provide the free and healthy physical conditions necessary for any sound upbringing. Early education will be largely 'negative', for it consists of 'protecting the heart from vice and the mind from error'. 'If man is good by his nature . . . it follows that he remains so as long as nothing alien to him changes him for the worse; and if men are wicked, as they are at pains to teach me, it follows that their wickedness comes from elsewhere; close the entrance to vice, and the human heart will always be good. On this principle I establish negative education as the best, or rather, as the only good one' (iv. 945). Although negative education is mainly preliminary, it constitutes a vital phase of the child's development, since it prepares the way for the eventual emergence of higher capacities by allowing the unimpeded development of the physical powers on which they depend.

If early education is mainly negative, it is certainly not inactive; from his very first years the child needs the freedom to express his developing energies. Even the baby seeks the unrestricted use of its limbs; from the very first months it shows that 'to live is not to breathe but to act—to use our organs, our senses, our faculties, all those parts of ourselves which give us the feeling of our existence' (iv. 253). The common habit of keeping the child in tight swaddling-clothes is already an anticipation of the imprisonment to which civil man will be subjected for the rest of his life. Negative education, therefore, prepares the child for the proper exercise of his primordial needs. 'I call negative education that which tends to perfect the organs, the instruments of our knowledge, before giving us this knowledge, and which prepares us for reason by the exercise of the senses' (iv. 945). If it does not produce virtues, it certainly forestalls vices; 'it does not teach truth but it saves from error; it disposes the child to everything that can lead him to the truth when he is in a position to understand it, and to goodness when he is in a position to love it' (ibid).

The reason for this confidence was already indicated in the Second *Discours* and is reaffirmed in *Émile*: it is the existence of 'the only passion natural to man': self-love or *amour de soi* (iv. 322)—a primordial and absolute passion which 'in itself is indifferent to good and evil', for it exists in its own right and precedes any kind of moral experience; it becomes good or bad by accident and according to the circumstances in which it develops. It provides the sole driving force behind every individual's existence and makes him what he is; 'it never leaves him as long as he lives and is the fundamental feeling of which the rest are only modifications.' It is not good or bad, because it appertains in the first instance to the individual's own existence and not to his relations with others. In its most rudimentary form it is little more than the impulse which impels the animal to self-preservation. However, as soon as it begins to develop, it reveals an expansive aspect; this is already discernible, according to Rousseau, in the child who spontaneously directs his affection upon those who minister to his needs. 'The child's first feeling is to love himself; and the second, which derives from the first, is to love those who are close to him' (iv. 492). When, in the mature human being, this expansive impulse is directed by reason and modified by pity, it can determine his attitude towards his fellow men and so lead to humanity and virtue. In its most developed form, 'self-love is good and always in conformity with order' (iv. 491); it thus develops from a very rudimentary feeling into a genuinely moral principle. *Amour-propre* or 'pride', on the other hand, is a relative, artificial feeling, originating in society and impelling every individual to attach more importance to himself than to others; it leads him to hurt his fellow men, for it springs from false reflection and from the habit of comparing himself with others; it originates in 'the first look which the individual casts upon his fellows' (iv. 523). *Amour-propre* is thus a disruptive, not a unifying, element in social relations.

Even a cursory glance at *amour de soi* and natural goodness shows that although these qualities are always present in man, they are not completely expressed at any particular moment, but gradually reveal their true character in the course of his development. Although the primordial form of self-love as self-preservation is an impulse known to all sentient creatures, in man it can assume new and more complex forms as it becomes associated with other impulses; from being a crude undifferentiated urge, it can be transformed into a highly developed feeling with special characteristics of its own. Human existence will thus pass through definite stages of development, each emerging from the preceding one while acquiring its own distinctive features.

Since life has an essential continuity and unity and yet passes through various phases with specific features of their own, it will form part of the universal scheme of things. The wise educator will recognize that the child has his own particular characteristics which make him what he is and, at the same time, that childhood is a phase of existence which can become truly meaningful only when it takes its proper place in the general order. 'Each age, each state of life, has its own particular perfection, the kind of maturity suited to it' (iv. 418). Yet this perfection has ultimately to be related to the whole movement of human existence from its primitive origins to its highest point of development. In the second *Discours* Rousseau had already called attention to the error of earlier thinkers who had failed to see that man was an evolving being and that in the state of nature he was not the rational moral being of social life. The same principle is applicable to the existence of the individual. The child is not a man in miniature; he is merely a potential man and, as such, does not yet possess the reflection and moral attributes of the mature human being. Educators have erroneously insisted on treating the child as though he could respond to the adult outlook. In fact, it is useless to reason with a child, insists Rousseau, because he has not the rational ability to follow an abstract argument; it is equally futile to overwhelm him with words, because he cannot grasp the concepts to which adult language refers. It is far more rewarding to try to see the child as he is in himself. In certain ways, for example, he resembles the savage: he is concerned with 'immediate physical interest'; he abandons himself entirely to his present being and pursues 'immediate, present advantage'; drawn to what 'touches' and 'interests him immediately', he exists in himself, enclosed to a large extent in the narrow circle of his own desires and feelings, incapable of foresight or disinterested curiosity (Cf. iv. 357–61, 363, 419). Since the child responds to his own spontaneous impulses, he relies mainly on his physical resources and instincts; he delights, like the savage, in his strength and energy, and once again we see Rousseau contrasting the vigour of the child and primitive man with the softness of modern man who is only too anxious to make his children as weak and effete as himself.

The main characteristic of the child's life, however, is not to be found in physical activity as such, but in its particular mode of expression. The child is happy because he is free; he enjoys 'the well-being of freedom'. The true character of this natural freedom has been misunderstood, thinks Rousseau, because it has been wrongly contrasted with the enslavement of civilized life; it has been too readily assumed that natural freedom is incompatible with any form of dependence. In an important passage,[1] Rousseau makes a distinction—which is to play a vital role in his political thought—between two kinds of dependence: there is first of all the false, irksome dependence which results from man's subordination to his fellows and their arbitrary will. This is an undoubted evil and the major source of human frustration and conflict; the child, like the man, will resent the rule of arbitrary authority and the 'capricious will of men'. On the other hand, there is another form of dependence readily accepted by both the child and the savage—dependence on these conditions do not create frustration, because they have an objective, impersonal character which causes them to be the same for all. In short, the individual will readily accept the constraints associated with objects, but not the irrational and unnecessary restrictions imposed upon him by human beings. 'It is in man's nature to endure patiently the necessity of things, but not the ill-will of other people' (iv. 320). It follows, therefore, that the expression of natural freedom is not incompatible with an acceptance of the harsh yoke of necessity and the laws of nature. The presence of a stable natural background may be an indispensable condition for the existence of a 'well-controlled freedom' (*une liberté bien réglée*).

It is significant that certain inescapable limitations to the human condition (such as sickness and death), which primitive man accepts without murmur, are a source of anxiety to civilized man who makes them the object of his restless reflection. Instead of relating sickness to nature, he attempts to invoke the help of doctors who merely make his condition worse than before. Medicine, affirms Rousseau, is more pernicious to men than all the ills it claims to cure (iv. 269), and all the more pernicious because any slight physical benefits it may bring (and they are very few) are greatly outweighed by its harmful psychological effects—cowardice, credulity, and fear of death. The obstacles involved in physical necessity are of a totally different kind and do not conflict with the basic impulse of self-preservation.

Although the child's early development consists mainly of the free

expression of his innate physical capacities, the educator's role is
clearly of the greatest importance, for it is he who is mainly responsible for harmonizing this natural growth with the acceptance of
physical necessity; it is his task to forestall the harmful effects of
arbitrary human will. Moreover, he will realize that the early extension of the child's experience already requires the development of new
mental and psychological aptitudes. Although the child has been
capable of some kind of rudimentary reasoning from a very early
period, it is only now that he begins to add memory and reason to
perception. As we have already seen, Rousseau does not treat reason
as an absolute, abstract faculty existing in its own right, but as a com-
posite faculty functioning with other human powers; its activity
depends largely on the particular level of existence at which it
operates. Since the child lacks the developed faculties necessary for
the proper exercise of reason, childhood may be described as 'the sleep
of reason' (iv. 344). Such simple rational operations as already exist do
not go beyond his reactions to his immediate environment, and involve no more than sense-experience. It is a question of *la raison
sensitive*, for it is limited to the relationship between the child's
sensibility and the objects around him. The only reason of which
we are capable in our earliest years is 'to know the use of our
strength, the relationship of our body to surrounding objects, the use
of the natural instruments which are within our reach and which
suit our organs' (iv. 369). *La raison sensitive* is directed mainly to the
use of feet, hands, and eyes, which are 'the instruments of our intelligence'. At a later stage it will develop into *la raison intellectuelle*
which involves a more abstract kind of thinking. 'What I call *la
raison sensitive ou puérile* consists of forming simple ideas through
the combination of several sensations; and what I call intellectual
or human reason consists of forming complex ideas by the combination of several simple ideas' (iv. 417). The adequate perception
of physical relations is a necessary preparation for relations of a more
intellectual kind. The psychological aspects of a rational function
which does not go beyond the child's concern with his own inner
needs and his physical environment will eventually assume (as Pro-
fessor Derathé points out)[2] a more metaphysical character as it
becomes associated with man's relationship with his fellow men, the

world, and God. Since, however, the proper use of reason is inseparable from the exercise of other faculties, it will develop slowly and find complete expression only at a later stage when the individual needs to establish relations with other men and base his conduct on reflection and conscience instead of mere impulse Although the child's use of reason obviously falls far short of the adult's, since it is limited to *les qualités sensibles* and their connection with the environment and self-preservation, it plays an important role in his life, for it helps him to give an active and meaningful expression to behaviour which, though animated by the vigour of natural freedom, might otherwise involve little more than a merely unthinking relationship with the objects of his environment.

Perhaps the most important aspects of this early phase of existence are its simplicity and purity. The purpose of negative education is to prevent the primitive self from being contaminated by contact with a corrupt environment. That is why Rousseau, as we have seen, is anxious to bring up Émile in the country and not in a town. Yet even at this early stage, the educator needs to exercise great vigilance, for it is only too easy to allow the child to be corrupted by the insidious influence of his immediate environment. In unfavourable circumstances his very weakness and dependence may make him a dominating imperious creature, especially when those around him give the mistaken impression that they exist only as instruments of his desires. If he were given the chance, such a child would rule the earth. Physical necessity is much more effective than the human will in compating this pernicious tendency to domination, for it confronts the child with an impersonal force that is impervious to his entreaties.

An education based on nature rather than human will has the great advantage of linking up the growth of the individual with the most fundamental aspects of the human condition. It is not a question of limiting his activity to some artificial role, but of seeing the progressive unfolding of his character as part of a larger process, and as a means of ultimately allowing him to take his place in 'the order of things' and the 'chain of beings' created by nature (iv. 308). If society is arbitrary, capricious, and artificial, the world, in the profoundest sense, is part of a vast ordered system. When human passions are 'ordered according to the constitution of man' (iv. 303), they allow him to find happiness and fulfilment in an attitude which reconciles the expression of his own innate capacities with the acceptance of his proper place in the universal scheme. This is why the educative process has eventually to be completed by the establishment of religious and political principles.

This fundamental notion of order shows that the particular characteristics of each phase of existence, though important in their own right, cannot be separated from the general movement of nature. The 'well-regulated freedom' of the child, which can be achieved only by his acceptance of the 'force of things' and the 'heavy yoke of necessity', expresses a kind of equilibrium between desire and capacity. If the child's desires are allowed to outstrip his capacities, he will experience frustration and discontent. Admittedly, this balance between desire and capacity, though essential for a time, cannot be maintained indefinitely, for he gradually becomes aware of new powers and desires. The incipient activity of his imagination, for example, can profoundly modify the course of his desires. Moreover, the growing complexity of the child's relationship with his environment stimulates activities which cause him to extend and expand his being. Although nothing can be more harmful than an idle curiosity for objects of knowledge which have no relevance or meaning for his immediate existence—and this is why Rousseau deprecates the premature acquisition of intellectual knowledge—the child can still have a healthy and genuine curiosity about his environment. In this respect, the development of curiosity is similar to that of reason, its precise form depending on the particular phase at which it operates.

The most significant aspect of the child's early mental and psychological growth emerges with the development of an active judgement which contrasts very markedly with the passive nature of sensation. Rousseau's view of this matter is much closer to Cartesian dualism than the materialist monism of Diderot and other *philosophes*. He believes that the individual can move outside himself and make judgements about the external world instead of being merely dominated by it. 'The distinctive faculty of the free and intelligent being is to be able to give a meaning to this word *is*' (iv. 571). This outward-looking movement and this power of conferring meaning on external objects are very different from the way in which contemporary social man is outside himself, for the latter simply derives his values from the opinion of others and imitates what is irrelevant to his inner life; the child's expansive feelings, on the other hand, are a natural movement unfolding from within and bringing into play faculties which relate him actively to his own emotional and mental needs and the demands of his immediate environment.

There is a rhythm in human development, involving an alternation between moments of inner concentration when man seems to be gathering his inner strength, and moments of expansion when he seeks to extend his being and move beyond himself to the outer world. With the approach of adolescence this expansive movement becomes more marked and the child 'casts so to speak into the future the superfluity of his present being' (iv. 427). There is a kind of superabundance of being which anticipates, albeit dimly at first, his future development. A decisive stage of his life will be reached when he realizes that instinct and bodily appetites are no longer adequate for his existence. After being concentrated within himself and dominated by his own desires, he gradually comes to feel other needs, to experience feelings for people rather than for mere objects. Hitherto he had treated other people as existing mainly for him; now he begins to see them as persons in their own right. At last he is ready for the experience of morality.

Notes

1. iv. 311. Cf below p. 101.
2. R. Derathé, *Le Rationalisme de Rousseau*, pp. 29 ff.

5

The Moral Development of the Individual

ROUSSEAU's account of the emergence of moral notions shows that they appear at a relatively late stage of the individual's development and in conditions which betray their complexity. An over-simplified view of Rousseau's moral ideas has perhaps been due to the excessive importance accorded to his eulogy of conscience and his criticism of reason. Essential though these principles are to a proper understanding of his moral outlook, they do not exist in isolation, but must be related to his other ideas on the subject. There is no doubt a sense in which Rousseau's moral philosophy is very simple, but this simplicity is characteristic of the unified and harmonious outlook of the fully developed and mature individual, and does not necessarily include the actual formation of his moral ideas. In *Émile* Rousseau points out that morality does not consist of simple notions imposed on the individual from the outside, but of principles originating in his own nature. At the same time, moral values do not exist in a void, but involve the co-operation of non-moral elements of the personality (such as reason) as well as its relationship with the environment. One of the thinker's main problems is to examine the interdependence of these various factors and to distinguish the essential features of moral experience from its merely incidental aspects.

Even though a complete description of moral experience requires an analysis of the personality as a whole, it is necessary to begin by recognizing that morality, like all basic human experiences, is rooted in sensibility; to discover its affective source we have to go back to man's most primordial characteristic—his *amour de soi*. Although this is absolute in as much as it is a primordial impulse depending on nothing but itself, it 'develops in accordance with the order and progress of our feelings and our knowledge, relative to our constitution' (iv. 523). *Amour de soi* does not remain a simple undeveloped impulse but gradually evolves and assumes more complex forms; in this respect, it follows the movement of nature, which is not just a primitive physical or biological force, but a 'well-ordered nature' (iv. 552). Rousseau frequently speaks of the order and progress of a nature that eventually attains a highly refined form of expression. In considering the child's developing sensibility, says Rousseau, it is essential to observe how 'the successive developments take place according to the order of nature' (iv. 501). However, the higher forms of nature emerge only slowly from earlier and simpler stages, so that man's original being, however complex its ultimate development, always remains grounded in his sensibility and feelings, rather than in a reason that achieves maturity only at a later stage of his existence. If, therefore, we are trying to find the source of morality, we must first consider its affective rather than its rational aspect.

The idea of the child as a self-sufficient being dominated by his immediate physical interests is perfectly valid for the early phase of human life when happiness rightly consists in the self's ability to become identified with the intrinsic possibilities of its immediate situation. Although this mode of existence has important implications for the later understanding of man (as does the loyalty of the savage to the intrinsic possibilities of his particular mode of being), it cannot serve as a model for the formation of the complete individual, since it does not go far beyond his relations with things. However attractive this self-sufficient life of instinct and feeling may be, it lacks any genuine moral quality, for it does not as yet bring the individual into contact with other people. It is only when he becomes involved with others that 'man begins truly to live'.

The appearance of this developing sensibility is linked up with the

expansive need of the human personality. This was much less prominent during the period of physical growth and was, in any case,
limited to the child's need to establish relations with things rather
than people. Yet even the child, as we have seen, is capable of some
kind of expansive affection, and the adult himself can respond to the
expansive possibilities of his sensibility. In an interesting passage of
the *Dialogues* Rousseau points out that sensibility is not a simple
innate impulse, but assumes two forms: physical and moral. Whereas
physical sensibility is concerned mainly with the satisfaction of
bodily appetites, moral sensibility expresses itself as a capacity for
satisfying emotional needs through a spontaneous attraction towards
(or recoil from) other people; whereas physical sensibility responds
primarily to objects and is concerned only with physical self-
preservation, moral or active sensibility enables us to 'attach our
affections' to other human beings. There is a spontaneous element in
our moral sensibility—a force of spiritual attraction analogous to the
attraction that is to be found between physical objects, but obviously
of a much higher quality. When this force acts positively, it is 'the
simple work of nature which seeks to extend and fortify the feelings
of our being' and is the source of 'all gentle and loving passions'.
This positive sensibility derives directly from *amour de soi* and is a
'pure matter of feeling in which reflection plays no part' (i. 805–6).
With the appearance of this expansive sensibility, therefore, the
individual experiences emotions which induce him to 'transport himself outside himself' (iv. 505). The 'expansive force of the heart'
impels him to look towards other people, and he feels 'this state of
strength which extends him beyond himself'. Once again, it is a
question of developing a primitive impulse and of following the progress and order of nature rather than of creating something completely new.

Perhaps Rousseau's concern with the idea of himself as a man of
sensibility causes him to over-emphasize this aspect of moral experience in his personal writings, but it is certainly in conformity
with his general view of the developing personality. Already in the
Discours sur l'inégalité he had called attention to the importance of
'natural pity'—'the first relative feeling which affects the heart
according to the order of nature' (iv. 505). Natural pity is the only

feeling which impels primitive man towards other beings. At this stage of human existence it is a blind, unreflective impulse, but it serves as the basis of more highly developed feelings and already has an expansive aspect. We are moved to pity 'by transporting ourselves outside ourselves and identifying ourself with the suffering creature', and 'by leaving our own nature, so to speak, in order to take on his' (iv. 529). Pity comes into play when the 'force of an expansive soul identifies me with my fellow men and when I feel myself so to speak in him'.

With the development of reflection and imagination, pity assumes a more complex form, and ceases to be merely instinctive: although it is still rooted in a natural impulse, it involves a certain reflection upon oneself and the co-operation of psychological factors other than those associated with mere feeling. Through the activity of imagination, memory, and reflection, I can make a more deliberate effort to relate another's suffering to my own inner self and vicariously identify myself with it. In the mature human being pity presupposes this capacity to enter—at least imaginatively—another's consciousness. However, this imaginative aspect is inseparable from memory, for I can feel genuine pity only for suffering of which I myself have also had some experience; imagination, memory and reflection combine to make me feel pity for the suffering of my fellow men. 'Indeed, how can we allow ourselves to be moved to pity, except by transporting ourselves outside ourselves and identifying ourselves with the suffering creature? by leaving, so to speak, our own being in order to take on his? We suffer only in so far as we judge that he suffers: it is not in us but in him that we suffer'. 'Nobody becomes sensitive to suffering except when his imagination is stirred and begins to carry him outside himself' (iv. 505–6). Yet pity alone cannot be the sole basis of morality, because it remains a mere impulse or feeling; it requires, as we shall see, the co-operation of other elements in the self if it is to acquire genuine moral significance.

The way in which adult emotions depend on the order of nature and its relationship with the progress of 'primitive affections' is also brought out by Rousseau's discussion of love, which reveals a similar process of development. Contrary to popular belief, love is not simply a spontaneous natural feeling, valid in its own right, even though it must originate in such a feeling. As Rousseau stresses in the second *Discours*, primitive man does not know love, being incapable of rising above a blind sexual impulse which allows no permanent attachments. Now adult love does indeed require a sexual element, and owes something to physical and psychological factors; men and women are first drawn together by an affinity of feeling and sensibility, and without this initial attraction, their relations with each other would never attain real depth or intensity. As Saint-Preux tells Julie, there is 'a certain unison of soul which is immediately discernible' and without these 'uniform ways of feeling and seeing' mutual affection would be impossible (ii. 125). Yet this spontaneous attraction is not enough to define true love. At its highest, love involves judgement and comparison and a deliberate act of choice; reflection as well as feeling is an indispensable component. Whereas sexual desire has a purely biological origin in so far as it involves little more than the desire of one sex to unite with another in a blind unheeding way, love is a feeling inspired by a specific object.[1] Whereas the sexual impulse is entirely unreflective inasmuch as it makes the individual concentrate on the immediate satisfaction of his own need, love has an artificial aspect, because it involves reflection and comparison as well as feeling and desire. Love, for example, is often associated with admiration and preference, and with a response to specific characteristics and qualities such as beauty, virtue, and merit. These reactions depend on capacities of which primitive man is quite ignorant. No doubt maturity of feeling creates serious problems too. The experience of sincere love has been made difficult, if not impossible, in the modern world by the baleful influence of the false passions generated by society as well as by the misuse of reflection; the corruption which has affected all human attitudes has inevitably exerted its influence on love, so that what is often described as love is only a grotesque parody of the real sentiment. Nevertheless, the experience of true love is impossible without the development of higher psychological and mental powers.

Modern life has also eliminated another essential feature of true love—reciprocity. Whereas blind sexual impulse is purely selfish, love has an expansive possibility which requires the active response of the other person. Yet this reciprocity has its dangers, since it is inseparable from reflection upon oneself and comparison with others. 'To be loved it is necessary to make oneself lovable—at least to the loved person' (iv. 494). This makes us compare ourselves with others and consider them as possible rivals, even enemies. In other words, the self-reflection which was present in pity is also active in love in spite of its different mode of expression. So a feeling capable of arousing the noblest aspirations can also lead to jealousy and aggression. In contemporary society love has assumed a degrading exclusiveness and egoism which owe more to opinion than to natural feelings. However, the misuse of human powers in no way impugns their essential value as a means of helping people to experience the reciprocity of genuine affection.

Yet another essential characteristic of love is the enthusiasm which not only provides it with its momentum, but also impels it beyond normal human limitations towards the ideal of perfection. 'There is no true love without enthusiasm, and no enthusiasm without an object of perfection, real or chimerical, but always existing in the imagination.' Maybe the subjective aspect of this idealistic aspiration makes true love a mere 'chimera, lie, and illusion'; 'if one saw what one loves exactly as it is, there would be no more love on earth' (iv. 656, 743). Nevertheless, the enthusiastic pursuit of perfection remains an indispensable element in love and inspires man with some of his finest feelings. 'Take away the idea of perfection and you take away enthusiasm; take away esteem and love is no longer anything' (ii. 86).

This idealistic and spiritual element has to take into account important differences between the male and female character. It is probably wrong to discuss the relationship of men and women in terms of some supposed equality or inequality or of trying to decide whether or not woman is inferior to man. Each 'attains nature's ends according to its own particular destination', but the perfection for which each strives can never be identical (iv. 693). Woman, insists Rousseau, is made especially 'to please man and be subjugated by him'. Although man must also please woman, it is only by his strength—that is a 'law of nature which precedes love itself'. Psychologically woman has a passive role which is expressed through her modesty and *pudeur*. Man's more aggressive approach to love, how-

ever, also has to take into account the fact that he will ultimately
depend on his companion. Even so, a typically feminine attitude
involves gentleness and submissiveness and the acceptance of the
inevitable constraints imposed on woman by her position as a dependent being; her eventual role as mother also commits her to a domestic
life. The existence of natural physical and psychological differences
does not constitute a barrier to the enjoyment of deep mutual affection,
so that 'from the coarse union of the sexes there are imperceptibly
born the sweetest laws of love' (iv. 697). One of Rousseau's constant
complaints against modern life is that it has destroyed the possibility
of love by failing to respect the essential differences between men and
women and by trying to reverse the role of the sexes, making woman
the dominant character and man her effeminate dependant.

In spite of the increasing complexity of moral development Rousseau insists upon man's need to be himself at every phase of his
existence: 'It is necessary to be oneself at all times and not struggle
against nature' (iv. 685). This, in turn, means that we must give ourselves 'entirely to each hour' and that every moment of our existence
must be marked by a genuine plenitude. Opinion is decisively rejected, because Rousseau considers it to be unnatural and based on
external criteria which prevent us from being ourselves; it 'makes
everything different and drives happiness from us' (iv. 691). On the
other hand, the power of opinion lies in its apparent objectivity and
inflexibility; what lies outside man seems more stable than his precarious inner life. Although nature's impulses are always right,
especially when they are pure and simple, they are not permanent.
Only the necessity of physical nature seems to outlast all the changes
in the lives of particular individuals. However satisfying the experience itself may be, natural emotion and spontaneous goodness are
apt to fade away. At this particular stage of his development, therefore,
man is faced with the problem of being himself and yet in conditions
which enable him to give stability and consistency to his feelings.
Moreover, he faces a further difficulty as his powers develop, for the
indefinite extension of desires is bound to reduce inner strength
(iv. 816). Even so, he can no longer accept the natural freedom of the
child or primitive man, for he has achieved a maturity and a capacity
for reflection which have taken him beyond mere feeling and physical

impulse; he requires more than the well-controlled freedom of physical necessity; he now has to find a new 'nature'.

No longer able to remain a self-sufficient being of unreflecting impulse, he is aware of the emergence of moral needs which presuppose a capacity for development and improvement. At first sight, these moral qualities may betoken weakness and insufficiency, for the individual, being unable to remain satisfied with his own being, begins to reach out towards other people. Man thus stands mid-way between the animal-like being whose nature is incapable of further change and remains identified with mere instinct and feeling, and the divine Being who exists by Himself and has no need of others. It is man's weakness which compels him to seek others and makes him sociable, but it is also his sense of insufficiency, his consciousness of not being all he could be, which causes him to move forward to a higher form of existence; it is only through his relations with others that he can achieve an adequate realization of his highest possibilities.

Man has to protect himself against weakness and inner conflict by the acquisition of a new strength, which ultimately involves a changed attitude towards others and, consequently, towards himself. Knowing the frailty of his own emotions, he seeks to fortify himself through the activity of his will. 'Man is weak by his nature, but strong by his will' (iv. 817). Had he not been brought into contact with others, he would never have been impelled to develop his will and and acquire inner strength. Ultimately the power of the will expresses itself as virtue, which presupposes man's capacity to resist his immediate impulses for the sake of some higher principle. True morality, therefore, shows that goodness alone is not an adequate basis for human existence. Rousseau points out that God alone is truly 'good' and the sole being who does not need to be 'virtuous'. The goodness of the man of nature, on the other hand, has to be supplemented by the will, and it is through the activity of his will that the individual becomes a truly moral being. 'I have made you good rather than virtuous', Rousseau tells Émile. This means that the young man's education is not yet complete, because 'goodness shatters and perishes under the impact of the human passions' (iv. 818). Émile's natural freedom will become increasingly precarious as he grows older, and happiness will elude him until he has learned to become 'free and master of himself'. 'Control your heart, Émile, and you will be virtuous.' Although every man is endowed with passions, whether he wishes to be so or not, it is his responsibility 'to reign over them' (iv. 819).

At the end of his pedagogic experiment, Rousseau thus reaffirms the moral principle already established in his very first *Discours* which, as we have seen, extolled the glories of virtue. There, however, virtue remained a rallying-cry rather than a clearly defined concept: the moral vigour of ancient republican heroes had been contrasted with the corruption and effeminacy of modern society. In *Émile* Rousseau tries to relate virtue to the development of the individual and to define its significance in the light of the complete personality. The activity of the virtuous will cannot be separated from other human powers and must eventually be related to the development of civil society. Émile has to be made to see its great importance in the last stages of his education, especially when he is being prepared for marriage. Yet even though Émile is quickly convinced of his love for Sophie, his tutor points out that his feelings for her are not a sufficient basis for marriage; he will never achieve a happy and stable relationship until he has learned to 'separate himself from his desires' and to set a certain distance between himself and the object of his striving; for the first time Émile is taught to resist nature for the sake of a higher good, which is natural in so far as it belongs to his possibilities as a complete moral being, but unnatural in so far as it presupposes a capacity for resisting and overcoming spontaneous feeling. No doubt, as Rousseau insists, man can be 'happy and free in the depth of the woods', but there he would be 'good without merit' instead of being truly virtuous (iv. 858). In this sense, therefore, virtue 'denatures' man because it requires him to resist his feelings and sacrifice his immediate interest to some higher good. On the other hand, it shows man that he has the strength and power to rise above the bondage of appetite and achieve a mode of existence denied to lower creatures.

If virtue requires strength, it may often involve a need to combat selfish impulses. In *La Nouvelle Héloïse* Rousseau does not hesitate to describe virtue as 'a state of war'; 'in order to live in it one has always to undertake some struggle against oneself' (ii. 682). He returns to the point in his last systematic statement of his religious beliefs—the letter to Franquières of 1769. 'This word virtue means *strength*. There is no virtue without struggle; there is none without victory. Virtue does not consist merely of being just, but of being so by triumphing over one's passions, by ruling over one's heart' (iv. 1143).

Without the help of the will, feeling would be powerless to inspire action. Thus the pity which is rooted in sensibility would not produce any moral result unless it were associated with the will: a man might feel pity for his fellows, but would take no steps to help them. Pity acquires a truly moral quality only when it is expressed as genuine beneficence. No doubt this beneficence would never come into being if it were not originally inspired by some strong natural impulse, but it would certainly remain sterile if it were not actively supported by the will.

Yet will, like feeling, cannot exist apart from other human powers. However important it may be, the will needs to be animated by feeling and enlightened by reason; only through reason can man acquire insight into the meaning of his actions and understand what he is doing. As we have already seen, reason is not capable of sustaining itself on its own resources and has to depend on something other than itself; but when the will operates in conjunction with reason, the individual comes to realize his existence as a being endowed with freedom—not the 'natural' freedom of the unthinking savage, but the 'moral' freedom of the mature man who has at last fulfilled the real possibilities of his being.

Likewise, will cannot remain a merely formal, abstract principle or the means of achieving some kind of impersonal ideal valid for its own sake. If will and virtue are inseparable from feeling, it is because they form part of a genuinely personal experience. Although virtue to some extent 'denatures' man (if by 'nature' we mean man's spontaneous innate impulses), it enables him to do his duty on difficult occasions when his immediate inclination might be to follow the promptings of selfish inclination; yet this does not mean that it separates him from his true 'interest'. As Rousseau told d'Offreville, moral interest certainly excludes 'selfish material interest', for the virtuous man is prepared to sacrifice, if necessary, not only his personal advantage, but even his life, for the sake of others; yet he still has to feel that such a heroic gesture is in accordance with his inner nature and the spiritual and moral interest which enables him to be himself. In all circumstances man has to be faithful to this higher self, even though this can be no longer identified with the natural happiness of primitive man. Virtue, therefore, is not synonymous with happiness in this simple sense and it does not give happiness, as the Stoics believed. On the other hand, 'it alone allows us to enjoy happiness when we have it'; it produces 'an inner satisfaction, a contentment with oneself' that can be attained in no other way.[2]

To some extent virtue must always remain precarious, for Rousseau is careful to point out, as Pierre Burgelin insists, that 'all virtues deteriorate without the help of wise prudence' (ii. 1269).[3] It is foolish to ignore the limitations of human nature or the benefits of modera-tion. 'To assume to each one his place and fix him in it, order the human passions according to man's constitution, is all that we can do for his well-being' (iv. 303). 'Let us not seek the chimera of perfec-tion', says Rousseau on another occasion, 'but the best possible accord-ing to the nature of man and the nature of society.'[4] This is indeed the advantage of seeing man's behaviour within the context of his being as a whole; the virtuous man does not exist by his will alone; he knows that he must acknowledge the reality of his feelings and reason and he understands his place in the complete order of things. The virtuous man cannot entirely escape the effects of his sensibility and the rational adult cannot overlook the importance of *la raison sensitive*, even though he has come to know the superiority of *la raison intellectuelle*. Man's existence is committed to a situation which involves his relationship with his own being, his environment, and the universal order; every aspect of his personality has to contribute to the harmony of the whole. At the same time, he can have justifiable confidence in his ability to fulfil himself in this way, for 'when he created man, God gave him all the faculties necessary to accomplish what he required of him' (ii. 683).

However essential it may be to man's moral fulfilment, virtue, being inseparable from interest in the highest sense, has constantly to find support in a feeling which is far deeper and more powerful than the transitory impulses of the natural man. If the individual is to love the good which his reason helps him to know and his will to choose, he has to rely on an inner feeling that can resist the sophisms of reason and the lure of selfish passion. Rousseau insists on the importance of inner feeling, because virtue has ultimately to be based on a need that is natural to the human heart and on the 'true affections of the soul enlightened by reason and which are an ordered development of our primitive affections' (iv. 523). It is a question of 'this *dictamen* which is more secret, more internal than the secrets of the heart, which cries out against merely selfish decisions' (iv. 1138). It is an 'inner voice' or 'inner light' which can set us on the path to truth and virtue when all else fails. This primordial feeling which originates in the depths of man's being is conscience.

It is significant that Rousseau's fullest account of conscience appears in his formal profession of religious faith, where it is described as a 'divine instinct'. The choice of term is important, for, in the first place, it shows that conscience is accepted as a primordial impulse or feeling which owes little to habit, and that it is the spontaneous expression of man's original and most intimate nature; in the second place, it is 'divine', because it belongs to the spiritual part of his being. Nature and religion combine to form this feeling which Rousseau calls 'the sacred voice of nature'. Conscience, therefore, is 'the voice of the soul', just as instinct is 'the voice of the body', and 'it is to the soul what the instinct is to the body' (iv. 595–8). It is the 'surest guide of an ignorant and limited being' who is also 'intelligent and free'. Its most remarkable characteristic is its infallibility, for it can impel man to virtue and righteous conduct when all else has failed. In a justly famous passage of the *Profession de foi du vicaire savoyard* Rousseau pays eloquent tribute to this 'immortal celestial voice' which makes us worthy of our Creator. Conscience is the divine spark within us—not some rare, freakish quality (even though it may seem so to men corrupted by the insidious influence of civilization), but the very essence of our nature as moral beings. If 'this divine moral sense' lifts us up to God, it also makes us aware of our fundamental humanity. When reason is involved in doubt and uncertainty, or the heart beset by unruly passions, conscience will never fail to succour those who listen to a voice that speaks 'the sweetest, purest and most energetic language of virtue' (i. 687). At such times man's wisest course is to heed this inner voice *dans le silence des passions*, for it will protect him against the promptings of his own selfish nature, the errors of reason, and the insidious influence of worldly maxims.

To those who desire an objective proof of the truth of conscience—and, in particular, Rousseau is thinking of those contemporaries who have been led astray by a materialistic philosophy that dismisses conscience and remorse as mere 'prejudice or chimera', and treats vice and virtue as the artificial products of environment, without any autonomous value—there is available the evidence of human nature: the 'manifest, universal agreement of every nation' and the 'remarkable uniformity of men's judgement' show that all people possess the same basic sense of right and wrong. What is more dishonest or futile, therefore, than Montaigne's pathetic efforts to unearth 'in some corner of the world a custom opposed to notions of justice'? How can some rare exception count against 'this principle admitted and recognized by the whole human race'? An impartial analysis of human reactions shows that 'behind the prodigious variety of judgements and opinions there persist the same ideas of justice and honesty'. Objective observation thus confirms inner conviction, and the man who trusts his conscience is following a principle 'written in the depth of his heart in indelible characters' (iv. 594).

Yet objective proof is unnecessary to the sincere individual who will not need to look so far, for, observing its power in his own life, he will discover that 'the voice of conscience speaks for itself'. It is in no way surprising to find Rousseau insisting that the power of conscience should be immediately evident to the inner self, when we remember that, in his view, conscience is a feeling rather than a judgement, and, as such, has the directness and simplicity of nature itself. Man does not need the 'frightening apparatus of philosophy' or 'the subtleties of reasoning' to prove the reality of an 'inner feeling' or 'voice' which every sincere human being can experience for himself and which cannot be permanently suppressed. 'The voice of conscience can no more be stifled in the human heart than reason in the understanding; moral insensitivity is just as unnatural as madness' (i. 972). As he says elsewhere, 'whoever obeys it, obeys nature'. Moreover, to the simplicity of its appeal must also be added the 'sublimity' of *cette sainte et bienfaisante voix* which evokes a heartfelt response in every man ready to make use of nature's most precious gift.

The apparently exceptional quality of conscience is due largely to the corruption of a society that has alienated man from his true self. Contemporary decadence makes it necessary for conscience to protect people against the vagaries of reason and passion, which have been made the instruments of pride and self-interest, and of that *amour-propre* which has everywhere usurped the authority of authentic *amour de soi*. In a regenerated society, on the other hand, conscience would be as natural and spontaneous as any other innate gift, co-operating with reason and freedom to secure the perfect fulfilment of the human being.

Because conscience is rooted in a feeling or instinct which moves us to love the good, it does not follow that it has any specific knowledge of the good. The principle which was applicable to the will is equally applicable to the conscience; conscience needs to be enlightened. Although innate feeling spontaneously impels us towards the good, it still needs to be cultivated. This is all the more important when we recall that the voice of conscience tends to be timid and, loving peace and seclusion, it is easily drowned by the noise of the passions; although its voice cannot be stifled, it may be silenced when it is in greatest need of being heard. To be fully effective, therefore, conscience needs the co-operation of reason. 'Reason alone teaches us to know good and evil. So conscience which makes us love the one and hate the other, although independent of reason, cannot develop without it' (iv. 288). 'To know the good is not to love it; man has no innate knowledge of it; but as soon as reason makes it known to him, his conscience impels him to love it; it is this feeling which is innate' (iv. 600). Conscience and reason thus support each other. Although conscience certainly provides the original impetus, the primordial urge, which makes possible man's awareness and pursuit of the good, it operates in conjunction with human powers, so that man can safely rely on his 'eyes, conscience, and judgement'; he 'has conscience to love the good, reason to know it and freedom to choose it' (iv. 605; ii. 683).

As the supreme expression of *amour de soi*, conscience seems to possess a strongly personal and subjective emphasis, but this is only partially true, for at the deepest level it brings the individual into contact with the principle of order; it has an objective as well as a subjective aspect, since it relates the individual to something greater than himself. In its highest form, *amour de soi* is no longer a merely spontaneous impulse, but a profound sentiment embracing various aspects of human existence. Not only has it a dynamic, forward-looking quality appropriate to the 'ordered progress of primitive passions' and the gradual expansion of all the inner possibilities of the personal self, so that through his conscience the individual is brought into a harmonious relationship with his own true being, but, as his personality develops, it becomes clear that spontaneous emotions, far from existing alone, have to be related to a higher principle of order. Man is no longer a separate being, for *amour de soi* is linked up with love of others. 'The love of men derived from the love of self is the principle of human justice' (iv. 523 n.). At first sight, conscience appears to be a simple, direct impulse, a profound feeling and an innate principle preceding all national and educational influences and impelling the individual to action by its own intrinsic power; it is 'an involuntary rule' which makes us judge all actions, whether our own or others, as good or bad. Yet this innate impulse involves other people as well as ourselves. Man may not be born with a primitive instinct of sociability, but he is 'meant to be sociable'. 'And it is from the moral system formed by this double relationship to oneself and to one's fellow-men that the natural impulse of conscience is born' (iv. 600).

The presence of conscience within the self and man's power to rise above the immediate promptings of instinct and passion reveal the active possibilities of his being. He does not passively obey the impulses of his bodily appetites but chooses to exist in accordance with some higher principle; this means that he is willing to relate his existence to a conception of order that goes beyond his immediate needs. Although it is animated by a deep feeling, his conscience expresses itself in acts. The voice of the soul enables the individual to triumph over the voice of the body, and establish an active relationship with order instead of being passively subjected to the senses. This also shows that 'self-love' is not a simple passion but contains at least two principles: an active intelligent one and a passive 'sensitive' one.

Conscience can thus be 'enlightened by reason, itself conducive to the acceptance of order'. 'Conscience develops and acts only with man's understanding; it is only because of his understanding that he comes to know order, and it is only when he knows this order that his conscience impels him to love it' (iv. 936). As Pierre Burgelin stresses, justice and virtue are only the moral aspect of the general principle involving 'the ordered progress of our primitive affections'.[5] In this way the individual comes to realize that he is no longer an isolated being but a part of the 'universal system' and 'the great whole'. It is only when he grasps this essential link between himself and the principle of order that he becomes capable of morality, for it is only then that he truly understands the complexity of his own being; the complete moral development of the individual leads him to acknowledge the necessity of establishing an ordered relationship with his own inner being, other men, and God. Self-love has now acquired a spiritual dimension which has lifted the individual above the appetites of the senses in order to make him aware of the link between the 'love of the soul' and the principle of order. Ultimately, therefore—and this is already obvious in Rousseau's account of conscience—the analysis of man's moral being has to be completed by a consideration of his religious destiny.

Notes

1. Cf. iii, 157–8; iv, 797–8.
2. *Corresp. complète* (ed. Leigh), ix, 143–8.
3. Cf. P. Burgelin, *La Philosophie de J.-J. Rousseau* (Paris, 1950), p. 355, where the quotations given in this paragraph are also to be found.
4. *Lettre à d'Alembert*, p. 148.
5. Op. cit., p. 99.

6
Religion

THE inclusion of the *Profession de foi du vicaire savoyard* in the fourth book of *Émile* not only stressed the significance of religion in the formation of the individual, but also gave Rousseau an opportunity of making a full and systematic statement of his own religious beliefs. His account of the composition of the work in the *Rêveries* shows that its significance went far beyond the pedagogic aims of *Émile* and constituted a decisive phase of his own intellectual and moral development. It was the result, he affirmed, of the 'most earnest researches ever made by any mortal' and could have been written only by a man who had always striven 'to know the nature and destiny of his being with more interest and care than he had ever found in any other man' (i. 1017).

Whether considered as a didactic treatise or a personal statement, the *Profession de foi* establishes principles which are in complete accord with Rousseau's conception of the order of nature already developed in the earlier part of *Émile*, but this order is now given a considerable extension of meaning and related to his conception of the universal system. If the individual can find true freedom only through the acceptance of principles 'written in the depth of man's heart by conscience and reason' (iv. 857), it is because the meaning of his existence depends on the eternal laws of nature and order created by God.

Since the question of order has to be referred to the more fundamental question of its originator, it is not surprising that Rousseau should be concerned with the problem of God's existence. On the whole, however, he is far less interested in proving God's existence as a truth valid in itself than in examining the question of His attributes. This preoccupation is already apparent in an early fragment which insists that the 'idea of God is inseparable from the ideas of eternity, of infinite intelligence, wisdom, justice, and power'.[1] It would be easier to eliminate the idea of divinity than to conceive of God without these attributes. At the same time Rousseau is anxious to safeguard the notion of God's transcendence. An early letter about Pope's *Essay on Man* (1742) sought to defend this principle by examining its relevance to the idea of the 'chain of being'—an idea that had figured prominently in Pope's poem. While affirming his acceptance of the notion of the chain of being and the universal order it presupposed, Rousseau had insisted that God, though the creator of the chain, stood outside it and that any consideration of His relationship to the world should not confuse the Creator and His work, time and eternity, the finite and the infinite.[2] Rousseau, therefore, was not prepared to subscribe to some vague form of pantheism.

The notion of the chain of beings and the main characteristics of God's creation is again taken up in Rousseau's letter to Voltaire on Providence (1756). Shocked by Voltaire's decisive rejection of the idea of divine Providence in his poems, *Sur la loi naturelle* and *Sur le désastre de Lisbonne* (the famous Lisbon earthquake of 1755 had given a great intellectual and spiritual shock to many thinkers of the time), Rousseau comes to the defence of Providence. He argues that particular physical evils must be interpreted in the light of the total scheme of things; men cannot reasonably expect the whole order of creation to be modified to suit their own petty needs. Every part is dependent on the rest and individuals may have to be sacrificed for the sake of the whole; particular evils, when seen within the context of the universal order, may prove to be good; in any case, physical elements do not have any validity in their own right, but derive their meaning from their place in the whole. Indeed, seen as a whole, the physical system will perhaps appear as 'necessary' rather than as 'good' or 'evil'. It is only to moral beings, endowed with freedom, that the term 'moral evil' can be properly applied. The problem of evil thus turns on the question of human freedom and its misuse rather than on a detailed consideration of the nature of the physical universe.

Nevertheless, neither human freedom nor the physical universe is self-explanatory, for their meaning is determined by their relation to an absolute Being—God, the unique source of all values. 'If God exists, he is perfect; if he is perfect, he is wise, powerful and just; if he is wise and powerful, all is good; if he is just and powerful, my soul is immortal' (iv. 1070; *RW*, p. 45). Rousseau doubts, however, whether any useful discussion of God's nature and attributes can be conducted merely 'by the light of reason'. The whole problem must be referred to a much deeper level of experience. Moreover, as he ponders the issue, Rousseau finds it impossible to avoid making a definite decision. Mere scepticism he finds intolerable both to himself and (as he believes) to most men.

I believe in God just as firmly as I believe in any other truth, because to believe and not to believe are the things in the world which depend the least on me; because the condition ofdoubt is a condition too violent for my soul; because when my reason wavers, my faith cannot remain long in suspense and determines itself without it; finally, a thousand subjects of preference draw me to the most consoling side and add the weight of hope to the equilibrium of reason. (iv. 1070-1; *RW*, pp. 45-6)

The same point was reiterated in the letter to Franquières of 1769.[3] The desire for certain principles, already present in his general philosophical outlook, is thus still more apparent in his discussion of religious issues.

Rousseau's view of God does not involve dispassionate intellectual reflection; he has little interest in producing elaborate metaphysical proofs of God's existence. His principal excursion into this field is to be found in the first part of the *Profession de foi*, but, as Masson has shown in his critical edition, this metaphysical demonstration probably did not form part of Rousseau's original intention and may have been prompted by his desire to meet the *philosophes* on their own ground; he perhaps wanted to provide an effective intellectual counterblast to their increasingly powerful support for philosophical materialism. His argument is based mainly on a consideration of matter in motion. Matter, he affirms, is not capable of generating its own motion, since it is essentially inert. (Rousseau appears to accept Descartes's mechanistic conception of the physical world.) Motion, therefore, must be due to an extraneous cause. Since this cause cannot be physical, it must be akin to will. God thus emerges as Supreme Will. The regularity of the laws of nature is a second feature of the universe and suggests that the creator is Supreme Intelligence. Finally, a consideration of human freedom and the dualism of mind and body—a theme to which we shall return—leads Rousseau to posit the principle of God's essential goodness.

When they are related to Rousseau's other references to God's existence, these metaphysical speculations do not seem to occupy a prominent place in his thought. He certainly holds fast to the idea of divine purpose, and even in his last systematic account of his beliefs—the letter to Franquières of 1769—he rejects the possibility of explaining the universe in terms of 'the sole play of matter and necessary movement'. Indeed, the activity of mind and judgement, as opposed to the passiveness of sensations, makes Rousseau look towards Cartesian dualism rather than contemporary materialism; he was always firmly convinced of the impossibility of reducing mind and matter to each other. The main interest of Rousseau's religious ideas does not depend on their metaphysical elements, but on his earnest attempts to relate them to the problem of human nature. Religion is important to man, because it concerns his 'original' being and helps to confer meaning on an existence which would otherwise be incomplete. This need to relate religious principles to man's whole nature perhaps explains why Rousseau attaches so little importance to mere rational proofs. Although, as we have seen, reason is an important human faculty, it does not function apart from the rest of the human personality. Moreover, it not only has to be reconciled with other factors such as conscience and feeling, but it also has to resist the baleful influence of passion and pride. The grievous state of modern culture is due to the subordination of reason to the false passions—

vanity, pride and opinion—generated by society. In order to free
reason from them, it is necessary to restore it to its true function,
which is not to generate truth from its own resources but to elaborate
and clarify the fundamental feelings or intuitions on which human
existence must ultimately rest. At times deep inner convictions will
provide a man with sound beliefs, even in the absence of convincing rational proof. It is interesting, in this connection, to see Rousseau
defiantly affirming his belief in God and immortality against the
arguments of philosophers. 'All the subtleties of metaphysics will
not make me doubt for a moment the immortality of the soul and a
beneficent Providence. I feel it, I believe it, I desire it, I hope for it,
I shall defend it to my last breath' (iv. 1075; *RW*, p. 51). *Corresp.
complète* (ed. Leigh), xv. 48. No doubt Rousseau does not usually find
it necessary to pitch his argument at this intense emotional level, but
he never ceases to stress the importance of inner conviction.

   The philosophical aspects of the physical universe as the ordered
system of a divine Creator are far less important than the spontaneous response of human sensibility to its spiritual essence. Already
at the psychological level Rousseau had insisted on the close connection between man's reactions to nature and his inner feelings; it
was not possible, he believed, for man to be satisfied with a merely
physical response to the external world. Of himself, Rousseau wrote:

I know how to see nature only in so far as I am moved; indifferent
objects are nothing in my eyes.... Trees, crags, houses, even men, are so
many isolated objects, each of which in particular gives little emotion to
the person who looks at it; but the common impression of all that, which
unites it into a single picture, depends on our condition when we contemplate it.... The various impressions which this country has made
upon me at different ages make me conclude that our relations always
have a closer connection with us than with things.[5]

As Pierre Burgelin points out,[6] this emotional reaction is largely due
to Rousseau's belief that beauty lies in the whole landscape, not in
its detailed features; it is the ordered system which reveals nature's
deepest meaning. Moreover, whereas reason tends to isolate and

analyse objects, sensibility and feeling are stirred by their general aspect and so are more prominent than reason in man's response to nature as a whole.

The more sensitive a contemplator's soul is, the more readily does he abandon himself to the ecstasies aroused in him by this accord [of natural beauty]. A gentle and deep reverie then takes possession of his senses, and he loses himself with a delightful rapture in the vastness of this beautiful system with which he feels himself to be identified. Then all particular objects elude him: *he feels and sees only in the whole.* (i. 1062–3)

At times Rousseau himself would experience an ecstatic identification with the beauty of the physical world; he would 'plunge headlong into the vast ocean of nature'. 'I feel inexpressible ecstasies and transports as I merge so to speak into the system of things and identify myself with the whole of nature' (i. 1065–6).

It was easy for Rousseau to make the transition from this affective reaction to a more definitely spiritual attitude in the presence of nature. In this connection it is sufficient to recall the striking passage in the *Confessions* where he describes his early morning devotions in the countryside at Chambéry. As he walked along, he prayed to God, not with a 'futile stammering of lips', but with a 'sincere elevation of heart to the author of the lovable nature whose beauties were before my eyes'. He never liked to pray in a room, but preferred to experience religious feelings in the midst of nature. 'I love to contemplate God in his works while my heart rises up to him' (i. 236). Sometimes his emotions would be so intense that he could do nothing but remain in a state of speechless adoration or else cry out 'O great Being'.[7] The external world was seen to have a divine origin because of its power to stir up powerful emotions in the soul of the beholder.

In the *Rêveries* Rousseau again refers to this deeper level of religious experience, but he also stresses that he was led to religion by a combination of various factors rather than by a single motive. 'Meditation in seclusion, the study of nature, the contemplation of the universe impel a lonely man to move upwards towards the author of things and to seek with a gentle anxiety the end of all he sees and the cause of all he feels' (i. 1014). Later in the same Promenade he reaffirms the essential basis of his religious attitude. 'Metaphysical quibbles and subtleties have no weight compared with the fundamental principles adopted by my reason, confirmed by my heart, and which all bear the seal of inner assent in the silence of the passions' (i. 1018). In matters which are beyond human understanding, however, mere intellectual objections cannot affect 'a body of doctrine so solid, so consistent and formed with so much meditation and care, so well suited to my reason, to my heart, to my whole being, and reinforced by the inner assent which I feel to be lacking in all other doctrines'. The reference to his 'whole being' is particularly significant, for it reveals the ultimate basis of his religious attitude: while no single element of the human personality when taken by itself can carry complete conviction, a belief that is supported by the whole of man's being commands immediate assent.

Rousseau's emotional reactions are associated with the idea of a correspondence or 'congruity' between inner and outer spiritual principles. Just as man himself is not a mere physical being, but is also endowed with a soul, so is the physical universe the creation of a spiritual being who has left evidence of his handiwork in what he has created. 'Vain arguments will never destroy the congruity which I perceive between my immortal nature and the constitution of this world and the physical order which I see reigning in it. I find there in the corresponding moral order, the systematic account of which is the result of my researches, the support I need to bear the miseries of this life' (i. 1018–19). As he told his friend Moultou: 'Nature is not inconsistent with itself; I see reigning in it an admirable physical order which never belies itself. The moral order must correspond to it.'[8]

It is especially within his own being that man finds the source of his religious beliefs. Considerations drawn from the order and beauty of the external world have always to be confirmed by 'inner assent'. It is significant, for example, that Rousseau's discussion of the notion of God as supreme will owes something to an analogy with the human will: the spontaneity of the human will is a striking example of the freedom which can communicate to inert matter a movement which it could not derive from its own resources. The second *Discours* had already indicated the importance of man's freedom, and Rousseau's whole conception of the individual's development was intended to culminate in a detailed consideration of the role of freedom in human life. The *Profession de foi* develops the point with reference to the power of will and judgement, which not only makes it possible to choose between truth and falsehood, but frees man from enslavement to his body. Freedom thus emerges as an ultimate and ineradicable aspect of man's being, a supreme human fact. 'The principle of all action is in the will of a free being; one cannot go back any further than this' (iv. 586; *RW*, p. 144).

It is interesting to note how Rousseau, after developing his two metaphysical proofs of God's existence in the *Profession de foi*, seeks to examine man's place in 'the order of things governed by God'; far more important than any objective metaphysical considerations is the argument derived from a consideration of human nature. A particularly striking feature of man's position in the world is the extraordinary contrast between the 'confusion and disorder of the human scene' and the 'harmony and proportion of nature'. This contradiction is due to the dualism of human nature which allows man misguidedly to reject what is for his own good, and to ignore the ordered beauty of the universal system. Foolish acquiescence in base and selfish desires leads a man to make his own existence the centre of the world, thus shutting him off from all that should extend and exalt his being. On the other hand, when he wills the good, he is drawn to the 'study of eternal truth, love of justice and moral beauty' as well as the 'regions of the intellectual world, the contemplation of which is the sage's delight'. If he looks within himself, he will also find a 'divine model', a simulacrum or 'inner effigy'—in other words, a spiritual ideal—which can inspire his actions in the world, for this model is grounded in the divine order which governs all things.

Now this is possible only because man is endowed with a freedom which enables him to make a sharp break in the system of physical necessity. This means, however, that he is not a simple entity, but a being who is free to choose the meaning of his existence; he can become master of himself and fulfil the spiritual and moral possibilities of his nature, or he can allow himself to be dominated and

degraded by his selfish passions. There are thus active and passive
elements in human nature—the active element being associated with
man's power of judgement and his ability to will and to choose, the
passive element revealing itself in his enslavement to the body and
its appetites. This is a point upon which Rousseau had always insisted
—that the mind is an active power, while sensations, being derived
from external objects, are always passive: at a higher stage of personal development, freedom itself emerges not simply as a mental
act, but as an activity of the will: I am free when I will to resist my
selfish passions; I am enslaved when I allow my freedom to be
subordinated to the influence of immediate desires.

Since freedom cannot be explained in physical terms, its existence
presupposes the presence of an immaterial principle in human nature.
The existence of freedom, in Rousseau's view, is inseparable from
the existence of the soul. Moreover, he considers it to provide one of
the most convincing arguments for the immortality of the soul, since
an immaterial principle that is independent of the physical world
must be indestructible and capable of surviving the dissolution of the
body to which, during earthly life, it remains attached.

Rousseau believes he is thus able to solve the problem of evil. Not
only does the idea of immortality allow him to justify the ways of
Providence, for an order which is disturbed in this life will be
restored in the next, but it also confirms the idea developed in the
letter to Voltaire on Providence that evil does not belong to the
universal system, but is the result of human action. There is thus no
problem of evil in any objective sense, but only the problem of moral
evil stemming from man's failure to make proper use of his freedom.
Even in man himself, evil does not spring from any deliberate desire
to do harm for its own sake, but from weakness or ignorance. In the
letter to Franquières, Rousseau transposes this into metaphysical
terms when he speaks of the 'eternal co-existence of two principles:
the active one which is God, the passive one which is matter and
which the active being combines and modifies with all its power, yet
without having created it or without being able to annihilate it'
(iv. 1142; *RW*, p. 390). Rousseau admits that the idea of 'creation'
raises great difficulties and he doubts whether the translators of the
Bible have properly rendered the real meaning of the original

Hebrew text. 'The idea of creation', he admits, 'confuses me and is beyond my grasp' (iv. 593). This question, however, is far less important than the human aspects of good and evil. That evil comes from weakness and limitation rather than from some objective source accords with Rousseau's conception of man's natural goodness. In his earlier works, it is true, he had stressed the idea that evil was largely the result of contemporary corruption, which had itself been due to man's having chosen the wrong historical path, but in his later writings he points out that human nature contains a principle of inadequacy, a kind of natural inertia which explains even the good man's failure to live up to his moral and spiritual ideals. The interesting description of the 'ideal' world in the *Dialogues* throws valuable light on the matter. He there insists that all primitive passions, being rooted in *amour de soi*, impel man towards happiness and that nature's true inclinations are always good; but goodness falls short of the virtue which requires us to control our feelings for the sake of some higher ideal; it is often necessary for us to 'fight and vanquish nature'. Now although we are not capable of doing evil for its own sake, we may be unable to summon up the strength necessary for the exercise of virtue. The habit of not resisting spontaneous impulse may eventually 'soften' the soul, so that evil is done through 'weakness, fear, necessity'. Such weak people (and Jean-Jacques admits he is one of them!) will never indulge in any deliberate effort to harm others and will know nothing of 'envy, treachery, deceit, and the other vices generated by society' (i. 671); but they will still fall short of the highest moral standards.

The chief difference between good and evil is revealed in the attitude towards order. The good man accepts his place in the universal scheme and is 'happy to direct himself in relation to the whole'; the wicked man, on the other hand, wants order to be organized around himself; he wants to be at the centre of the universal order instead of remaining on its circumference. Such an attitude is as foolish as it is unthinkable, for a complete reversal of the universal scheme can never be made for the profit of an individual, or even of humanity itself. In any case, there is no need for uncertainty or confusion in moral questions, for as soon as the individual rises above the influence of selfish interest, he is aware of the innate principle of justice and virtue which, as we have seen, is identified with the power of conscience.[9]

Simple and few though they are, Rousseau's fundamental religious notions are, in his opinion, the only dogmas required by any genuine 'natural religion'. Religion is natural because it is based solely on the evidence of innate human capacities. 'The good use of their faculties', especially their 'eyes, conscience, and judgement', shows men that God has revealed himself through 'his works' and 'their hearts'. To find religious truth the individual has only to look inwards at his own being or outwards to the 'universal system'. 'See the sight of nature, listen to the inner voice' (iv. 607; *RW*, p. 168). The essential simplicity of these principles is further explained by the fact that man's proper exercise of his faculties will lead him to seek only those truths which 'interest' him and which 'it is important for him to know' (iv. 592). These expressions, so frequent in his philosophical discussions, are equally prominent in the exposition of Rousseau's religious ideas and are in conformity with his statement: 'I shall never reason about God, except when I am forced to do so by the feeling of my relations with him' (iv. 581). He will seek only those religious ideas which are 'interesting' to him. Although, as we have seen, 'interest' involves men's moral and spiritual rather than his physical being, it does not go beyond the limits of human nature. All this follows logically from Rousseau's initial assumption of natural goodness, which provides the basis of an optimistic acceptance of man's ability to effect his own salvation. 'If I exercise my reason and cultivate it, if I use the immediate faculties which God gives me, I shall learn of my own accord to know and love him, to love his works, to will the good which he wills, and, in order to please him, to fulfil all my duties on earth. What more can I learn from all the knowledge of men?' (iv. 625). The reasoning of other men, dominated and perverted by *amour-propre*, can add nothing to the sincere use of my own mind and will almost certainly lead me astray. 'Everything that a man knows naturally, I too can know, and another man may be as mistaken as I' (iv. 610; *RW*, p. 171). Nobody can ultimately avoid the responsibility of having to judge for himself, and decide the meaning of his own existence.

Rousseau's defence of nature as the basis of religious truth naturally brought him into conflict with both *philosophes* and theologians. Although his religious ideas were not particularly original in themselves, their very simplicity and earnestness made them unacceptable to thinkers who had decisively rejected a supernatural interpretation of human nature. Rousseau himself saw his defence of religion as the main point of disagreement between himself and the *philosophes*. Although his description of them as 'ardent missionaries of atheism' may have been exaggerated—not all *philosophes* shared the aggressive anti-religious attitude of a Baron d'Holbach—it is true that religion as a personal experience had little significance for thinkers like Voltaire and d'Alembert, to whom Rousseau's advocacy of spiritual values must have seemed either quixotic or offensive. On the other hand, his enthusiastic support of natural religion brought him into sharp conflict with all defenders of revelation and traditional ecclesiastical authority. Since man, in Rousseau's opinion, can find God by his own efforts, not only is any kind of intermediary unnecessary, but it may serve as an insuperable obstacle to the discovery of truth. 'How many men', laments the Vicaire, 'between God and me!' (iv. 610) The characteristic Christian doctrine of the Incarnation was thus irrelevant to Rousseau's natural religion; the idea of a Church claiming unique and infallible authority was also rejected on the grounds that such a notion falsely presupposed that members of a particular ecclesiastical organization had a source of truth denied to the rest of mankind.

Apart from this general rejection of revelation as either a superfluity or a hindrance, Rousseau's criticism of traditional orthodoxy is in accord with the *philosophes'* outlook in another respect: claims to unique revelation and authority inevitably lead to bigotry and fanaticism. Rousseau is convinced that religious ideas, like all others, have been corrupted by the influence of society, which incites men to intolerance and fanaticism. Any claim to the exclusive possession of religious truth is usually accompanied by a desire to satisfy the most selfish and ferocious passions. Theologians, like philosophers, are particularly susceptible to the influence of pride and vanity, and seek constantly to dominate other people's minds. Religious intolerance is worse than other kinds, because it is found in men whose lives are supposed to be devoted to the service of Christian love.

Of the various forms of human authority the most insidious, in Rousseau's view, is the one which relies on books. Authentic religious education, like all education, can never be effectively based on books, for these merely perpetuate the errors of *amour-propre*. To look for truth in the printed word is to become lost in the myriad of competing views and systems by which men try to impose their will on other people. Books, like other forms of authority, are the product of a corrupt social environment, and, in a still more general sense, reflect all the limitations of the social and historical process: pride, envy, love of power, these and other vices are characteristic of a society which has sacrificed *amour de soi* to the claims of *amour-propre*. Reliance on bookish authority is a sign that man has once again abandoned the lessons of nature for the illusions of opinion. It is thus not surprising that the Vicaire should declare that he has closed all books in order to open 'the great and sublime book of nature' (iv. 625). This, in Rousseau's view, is the only authority in which man can place absolute trust and the only means through which he can hope to recover the simplicity of authentic religious experience.

Rousseau's condemnation of bookish authority in religious matters does not include the Gospels, which, he affirms, have the unique merit of expressing the principal qualities of natural religion; they contain a 'simplicity' that wins the immediate approval of reason and a 'sublimity' that appeals directly to the heart; nothing can equal the 'majesty' and 'holiness' of a book whose dogmas are so simple and morality so sublime. The constant application of the two epithets, 'simple' and 'sublime', to the Gospels suggests that the biblical message is in perfect harmony with the conclusions of reason and nature. But this also means that the Gospels must not be treated primarily as historical evidence; 'this sacred book' is remarkable for the rationality and sublimity of its teaching rather than for the uniqueness of the events it describes. Its undoubted historical veracity is not guaranteed by the approbation of any external authority, but by its ability to satisfy our reason and conscience; the immediate, spontaneous assent of our inner being to the Gospel message is enough to convince us that it cannot have sprung from human imagination. In other words, the validity of the Gospel is not based on historical facts and evidence but on the irrefragable testimony of human nature. Admittedly, historical considerations may help to strengthen our inner conviction. For example, an examination of the outlook of Jesus' Jewish contemporaries clearly shows that they could never have discovered principles which were beyond their comprehension. History, however, merely supports the conclusions of nature; it can never be authoritative in its own right or run counter to the lessons of nature. Ultimately it is reason and conscience, not history, that provide us with adequate criteria for distinguishing between truth and falsehood. Our understanding of any religious text involves 'a submission to the authority of God and reason, which must precede that of the Bible, and which serves as its foundation' (*Corr*. viii, 237). Inevitably, therefore, it is man's natural powers and 'the unalterable order of nature', not some arbitrary authority, which must determine his final attitude towards the Bible.

The fact that nature, not human authority, is the ultimate religious criterion means that even an exceptional work like the Bible cannot be exempt from criticism. Sublime though it is, it is still a book and, as such, not free from human error and weakness. In spite of its sublimity, 'this same Gospel is full of incredible things, of things which are repugnant to reason, and which it is impossible for any sensible man to conceive or to admit' (iv. 627; *RW*, p. 190).

The need to test religious ideas by the principles of nature and reason explains Rousseau's aversion to the idea of revelation as a privileged way to religious truth and his scepticism on the subject of miracles. Many of the miracles recorded in the New Testament must belong to that category of 'things that are repugnant to reason' and the mind of 'any sensible man.' Rousseau believes that they can add nothing to the testimony of natural evidence, and may in fact merely confuse or repel those who are ready to respond to the simplicity and sublimity of the Gospels. Why should God need to have recourse to phenomena which run counter to the laws of the universe he has created, when the most impressive truth will always be 'the most common, the simplest, and the most reasonable'? Since our main ideas about God himself are based on nature alone, why should we need to invoke some supernatural authority to confirm them? This is the main burden of Rousseau's argument about miracles—that they are quite superfluous as supporting evidence for the truths of natural religion; they can add nothing to proofs based on the evidence of our 'own faculties'. In any case, to speak of the miraculous quality of any phenomenon lying beyond our rational comprehension is surely to make a rash assumption, since it presupposes a complete knowledge of the laws of nature. According to Rousseau, the progress of science is constantly transforming alleged miracles into commonplace truths.

However, the compelling force of the Gospels does not rest solely on their 'elevated pure morality'. The striking personality of Jesus himself—a unique example of a man living out the truths he so fearlessly teaches—gives them powerful and convincing support. Particularly remarkable is the contrast between Jesus as the embodiment of 'the simplicity of the most heroic virtues' and the Jews as an example of 'the basest nation' of their day. The greatness of Jesus becomes especially obvious when he is compared with one of the most respected philosophers of antiquity, Socrates. The latter undoubtedly died like a sage, nobly and courageously, but without great pain and supported until the very end by the admiration and affection of his friends; even as a philosopher he invented nothing, since he drew on the wisdom of his predecessors; had it not been for his honourable death, says Rousseau, Socrates would probably have been known to posterity as a mere sophist. If the Greek philosopher drew strength and knowledge from his environment, Jesus had no such force to help him: he was alone in a hostile world. 'From the heart of the most furious fanaticism the highest wisdom made itself heard.' Still more horrible and heart-rending was the manner of his death as a criminal expiring in torment, 'insulted, mocked at, cursed by a whole nation', and yet praying to God for the salvation of those who were putting him to death. 'Socrates taking the poisoned cup blesses the man who offers it to him with tears; Jesus, in the midst of frightful torment, prays for his merciless executioners' (iv. 626; *RW*, p. 190). In a famous sentence Rousseau sums up the essential difference between the two: 'Yes, if the life and death of Socrates are those of a sage, the life and death of Jesus are those of a God.' But this comparison is meant to show Jesus' superiority over Socrates; it does not imply an acceptance of his divinity. For Rousseau Jesus was no doubt unique, but as a 'divine man', not as the Son of God. He was not the God–Man of orthodox Christian tradition, but a perfect example of nature's noblest qualities.

At times Rousseau can wax eloquent, even sentimental, over the figure of Jesus: in the third of the *Lettres écrites de la Montagne* he describes Jesus' morality as having 'something attractive, seductive and tender' and his character as being that of 'a man of good society' with a 'sensitive heart'. 'If he had not been the wisest of mortals, he would have been the most lovable' (iii. 754). That Rousseau considered Jesus as the founder of natural religion and the remarkable embodiment of its human qualities is also revealed by a curious tendency in his later years to see himself as a Christ-like figure, for was not Jean-Jacques also—though to a lesser degree perhaps—a remarkable example of the good man persecuted by a wicked world?

If we acknowledge Jesus' authority, it is because of the way in which he exemplifies authentic human qualities which make an immediate appeal to our conscience and reason. According to Rousseau, the error of Jesus' contemporaries and successors was to have forgotten this simple but vital fact. Already the principles of natural religion as advocated by Jesus were corrupted by St. Paul and, later, by the Church. In at least one place Rousseau stresses that Jesus' first intention was to raise up his own nation and make it a free people (iv. 1146; *RW*, p. 394). As the eighteenth-century *philosophes* also believed, Christianity, for Rousseau, represents the history of men who gradually abandoned or misrepresented the teachings of its founder. Indeed, if Jesus himself was unique as a person, his message was essentially rational and human in its emphasis. This is precisely what the Church has forgotten. The truth is that we should recognize 'a more than human virtue in his conduct' and 'a more than human wisdom in his lessons' (iii. 698–9).

Rousseau's emphasis upon the virtue and wisdom of Jesus is in complete accord with his fundamental views about the goodness of the universal order. Jesus' role is to help man to understand his own true nature and to find his proper place in the general order of things. If supernatural grace and the idea of the Incarnation can add nothing to man's search for spiritual fulfilment, it is because there is no need for him to try to modify the universal order. Rousseau condemns the idea of supplicatory prayer as unnecessary and presumptuous; there is only one true prayer: 'Thy will be done.' Why should men wish to disturb the whole order established by God's wisdom and maintained by his providence? To ask God to alter his creation for our own petty sakes is absurd. Our true attitude should be one of admiration and adoration. 'I converse with Him,' says the Vicaire, 'I imbue all my faculties with His divine essence; I am moved by His benefits; I bless Him for his gifts, but I do not pray to Him. What should I ask Him for? That He should change the course of things for me, that he should perform miracles in my honour?' (iv. 605). The order of the universe is the ultimate reality towards which all men's aspirations should be directed without any thought of their own selfish advantage. Rousseau's religious system thus seems to culminate in an emphasis on the notion of spiritual order and man's need to respect it. The Vicaire concludes the exposition of his natural religion by calling attention to his habit of indulging in 'sublime contemplations'. 'I meditate upon the order of the universe, not in order to explain it by vain systems but in order to admire it constantly, to adore the wise author who makes himself felt in it' (ibid).

Nevertheless, the principle of order does not stand as an isolated impersonal principle; it is something which the individual 'loves' and from which he derives the meaning of his existence. Moreover, human existence, though created by God, is not based solely upon the principle of order but is valuable for its own sake. If Rousseau lays great stress on the notion of immortality, it is because it allows him to anticipate the experience of complete personal fulfilment in the next world. 'I aspire to the moment', insists the Vicaire, 'when, delivered from the shackles of the body, I shall be *myself* without contradiction, without division, and shall need only myself in order to be happy' (iv. 604–5). No doubt in the afterlife we shall not be completely alone, for 'we shall enjoy the contemplation of the Supreme Being and the eternal truths of which he is the source, when the beauty of order will strike all the powers of our soul' (iv. 591), but we shall also have a perfect experience of our own being.

We shall know a condition of 'happiness, strength, and freedom', and the 'supreme felicity' of being ourselves. The contemplation of God's order will be accompanied by an equally strong sense of our own reality. This is already the source of our earthly satisfaction in the contemplation of God's creation. 'I acquiesce in the order he establishes, certain that I myself shall enjoy this order one day and find my felicity in it, for what sweeter felicity can there be than to find myself part of a system in which everything is good' (iv. 603; *RW*, p. 163). Yet there is a particular happiness to be found in the feeling of one's own personal existence, as Rousseau indicates on several occasions in the *Profession de foi*. The highest degree of happiness is the glory of virtue and the consciousness of one's own essential being. 'Supreme enjoyment is in contentment with oneself; it is to earn this satisfaction that we are placed on earth and endowed with freedom, tempted by the passions, and restrained by conscience' (iv. 587; *RW*, p. 145). A little later he speaks of the 'pure pleasure' which 'springs from contentment with oneself' (iv. 591; *RW*, p. 149). The good man will thus find ultimate happiness in the enjoyment of his own nature and in existing in accordance with the principle which makes him what he is. This is true at every level of human experience. It is to be noted that although Rousseau's letter to Voltaire attempts to refute by means of reasoned arguments Voltaire's objections to the goodness of God's creation, it lays even greater stress on the notion of existence. Whatever may be the theoretical conclusions drawn by pessimists from the pain, cruelty, and injustice of human life, Rousseau points out that most men find in the mere fact of their existence a satisfaction that outweighs the effects of all their sufferings and misfortunes; in spite of the most adverse circumstances, existence is felt to be valuable in its own right. Whereas Providence has arranged for the position of every material being to be determined by its relation to the whole physical system, in the moral sphere the value of every intelligent and sensitive being is grounded in its own existence. Since man is a moral and spiritual agent, the ultimate meaning of his being does not depend on his body or physical environment, but upon the free acceptance of a personal and intrinsically valuable existence. Furthermore, as has already been pointed out, freedom presupposes the presence of a spiritual element in man, so that the mere enumeration of physical evils, however many or dreadful, can never impugn the spiritual and moral basis of his being. It is better for man to exist than not to exist, whatever the particular evils and limitations of his material condition; to exist according to his own nature is his greatest privilege, and this supreme fact overshadows all the rest.

Notes

1. iv. 1033 (*RW*, p. 8). All the religious texts mentioned in this chapter are to be found in my edition of *Rousseau's Religious Writings* (Oxford, 1970), quoted hereafter as *RW*.

2. *Corresp. complète* (ed. Leigh), i. 132–43 (*RW*, p. 20).

3. Cf. above, p. 8.

4. Cf. *Profession de foi du Vicaire savoyard*, ed. P.-M. Masson (Paris–Fribourg, 1914).

5. *Corresp. complète* (ed. Leigh), xv. 48.

6. Op. cit., p. 154. Cf. also below, pp. 123f.

7. Cf. the third letter to Malesherbes, i. 1141 (*RW*, p. 105).

8. *Corresp. générale*, xix. 89.

9. Cf. above, pp. 64–69.

7
Political Theory

With the elaboration of his religious principles, Rousseau completes the exposition of his general ideas, for the individual has at last been made aware of the real meaning of his existence and his place in the 'order of nature'; he has discovered the absolute values inherent in his relationship with God, the universe, and himself. Nevertheless, these principles leave unresolved one very important problem—the precise nature of his relationship with his fellowmen and his participation in the social and political order. Émile has been brought up as an individual, but, as Rousseau acknowledges, he has yet to become a citizen and a member of the body politic. That is why the last book of *Émile* contains a summary of the political ideas elaborated in the *Contrat social*: Émile must take his place in the civil order as well as in the order of nature. It would no doubt be possible to analyse the notion of virtue and justice in accordance with the 'nature of things and independently of human conventions', for all justice comes from God and 'universal justice emanates from reason alone',[1] but such ideas remains merely abstract until they become part of man's relations with his fellow men. No philosophy of human nature can be complete until it has examined the problem of the individual's membership of civil society. This idea does not mean, as many critics have supposed, that Rousseau's political and social ideas are necessarily inconsistent with the rest; they simply deal with a field of experience which has its own particular problems and characteristics.

Rousseau maintains that the individual's confrontation with other people and with the need to find a common basis for a peaceful and happy life together constitutes one of the decisive turning-points in his development, for, as we have seen, morality appears only with the advent of society. The solitary and independent existence of primitive man in the state of nature precludes any possibility of moral relations, because it rests entirely on physical and instinctive impulses; it is only when he is brought into close contact with his fellow-men that the individual develops powers which are merely dormant at the primitive stage. *Amour de soi* can no longer remain a vague feeling absorbing the individual's entire being, for the development of the self involves the establishment of new relationships which affect its internal structure as well as its reactions to the outside world; the conscious exercise of new powers such as reason, will, and conscience is accompanied by a need to look outwards towards other people. No longer satisfied with the natural freedom of the solitary being, the individual will henceforth base his existence on the acceptance of a certain human order, and it is on this principle also that morality must ultimately depend. 'These words "virtues" and "vices" are collective notions which originate in human intercourse' (ii. 971). Through our participation in social relations, we learn, as Rousseau says in his *Dialogues*, that 'our sweetest existence is relative and collective and our true self is not entirely in us. Such is man's constitution in this life that he never succeeds in truly enjoying himself without the help of other people' (i. 813).

If morality presupposes the principle of order, it also requires another equally important human activity—freedom. Whereas natural freedom is quite compatible with the existence of physical nature, because it is based on self-preservation tempered by pity, true human freedom, as we have seen, can emerge only at a higher stage of human existence when man has acquired the capacity for deliberate choice. When he comes into close relationship with his fellows, he is no longer a creature of blind impulse, but a reflective being who not only sees himself as the object of his own and other people's 'look', but also chooses, by a deliberate act of will, to adopt a particular attitude towards the world. *Amour de soi* still dominates his existence, but it now assumes a more complex and reflective form, for it belongs to a being whose behaviour is directed by will and reason rather than by mere feeling. Rousseau does not doubt that this higher form of freedom is man's most precious and distinguishing characteristic; no way of life can be acceptable which fails to respect this essential attribute. 'To give up one's freedom is to give up one's being as a man, the rights of humanity and even one's duties. There is no possible compensation for anyone who gives up everything. Such a renunciation is incompatible with man's nature and to remove all freedom from his will is to remove all morality from his actions' (*CS*, I. 4; iii. 356). The main problem, therefore, is not to establish the basis of social relations but to determine how the freedom of the individual can be reconciled with that of other people.

The priority accorded to freedom has far-reaching effects upon the elaboration of Rousseau's political principles, for it leads him to stress at the very outset that the only political society acceptable to man is the one which rests on general consent. In spite of important differences between Rousseau and earlier liberal thinkers, they are in complete agreement on this initial point: every valid political society must be based on the free participation of its members. Rousseau points out that this assumption is required by 'natural right', in so far as the suppression of freedom violates man's essential nature. This stress upon freedom also explains his use of the traditional idea of the 'social contract', an idea that had been given considerable prominence by political thinkers from the sixteenth century onwards, and especially by those who were anxious to combat the political absolutism embodied, for example, in the theory of the Divine Right of Kings; contractarian thinkers maintained that society is brought into being by a definite act of will and by a deliberate choice on the part of all its members. If Rousseau draws very different conclusions from this premiss, it is mainly because of his different conception of the meaning of 'natural right', but he never doubts man's need to exercise his freedom and will in the formation of the civil association.

This priority accorded to freedom as the basis of political life causes Rousseau to reject two traditional explanations of the origin of political society. In the first place, political authority cannot be based on force, because force can never constitute a 'right', physical power and morality being two entirely different concepts. Rousseau criticizes very severely the Natural Law School thinkers, especially Grotius and Pufendorf, for having tried to smuggle this assumption into their ideas: they had argued that a captive people could agree to accept permanent enslavement in return for its life. No such agreement is possible, argues Rousseau, for enslavement, being based on nothing but physical power, will last only so long as it can be enforced. In the second place, society cannot be explained as a natural phenomenon, that is, as the result of man's innate sociability. Man has no innate sociability, but only certain powers which impel him to enter into close relationship with his fellow men when he chooses to do so. The formation of society depends on rational choice, not spontaneous feeling. That is why Rousseau rejects any possible analogy between the society and the family: the father's authority is based on the physical dependence of his children who assume their own freedom as soon as they reach maturity; any subsequent paternal authority requires their free consent.

It is this stress upon freedom which induces Rousseau to establish an indissoluble link between politics and morality. As the expression of man's freedom, political society naturally involves the moral attributes essential to all valid forms of freedom. 'It is necessary to study society through men and men through society', declares Rousseau: 'those who wish to separate politics and morality will never understand anything of either' (iv. 524). Although the individual is still faced with the responsibility of achieving virtue and moral freedom in his own personal life, he can no longer do so in isolation from other people. It is only through participation in the complex and decisive relationships of social and political life that he can understand the full significance of moral issues. The role of society is thus decisive: it is only in society that man can be transformed from a 'stupid and limited animal' into a 'free intelligent being' and so escape from 'the bondage of appetite' to enjoy the experience of justice and right.

Nevertheless, the link between morality and society involves special problems, since the individual cannot be left free to determine

his own unrestricted relationship with his fellows; rightfully concerned with the protection of his freedom, he none the less has to
acknowledge his need to relate it to a conception of order which will
allow other people to secure the effective exercise of their freedom.
The specific problem of political order will thus involve the establishment of conditions which permit all members of society to participate
on equal terms in a civil association based on the principle of freedom.

There is a further consideration: although political freedom always
presupposes a large measure of moral autonomy and the exercise of
will and judgement, it cannot function in a void, but has to reckon
with the formative influence of the environment. In the same way, the
educator, while trying to bring up his pupil in accordance with the
principles of 'nature', must help him to establish a sound and healthy
relationship with his surroundings; even though Émile's early education is largely negative, since it is concerned mainly with protecting
him from corrupting influences, it still requires him to establish an
active relationship with objects; it is not until he attains maturity that
he will be able to control this environment in a more rational way
and adapt it to his needs as a moral being. The deliberate organization
of the environment will constitute a decisive moment in his personal
and civic life. It will be recalled that one of Rousseau's unfulfilled
projects was the composition of a work he proposed to call *La Morale
sensitive ou le matérialisme du sage* (*The Morality of Sensitivity, or
the Materialism of the Sage*). Man's unhappiness being largely due to
his inability to adapt himself to the conditions in which he lives,
Rousseau proposed to develop principles which would enable the
'animal economy' to function in harmony with the various physical
factors that were brought to bear on it; the individual's soul would be
in 'the state most favourable to virtue' if his moral life could be
helped, rather than obstructed, by physical conditions such as climate,
seasons, colours, and sounds. This consideration would become all
the more important when due attention was paid to the great influence exerted by the physical world upon the formation of feelings and
emotions as well as upon bodily sensations (Cf. i. 408–9).

The same principle operates, though perhaps in a different way, at
every level of man's existence, as Émile's education makes clear.
Political freedom is to a large extent dependent upon an environment

that will give it effective expression. In the *Confessions* Rousseau wrote: 'I had seen that everything depended radically upon politics and that, however one set about it, no people would ever be anything but what the nature of its government made it be' (i. 404). 'It is certain', he insisted in his article 'Économie politique', 'that men are in the long run what the government makes them to be.' The preface to the play *Narcisse* reaffirms the same point: 'Every vice belongs not so much to man as to man badly governed' (iii. 251; ii. 969). Again the parallel with the education of the individual is plain: although he is meant to become a free and responsible being, his existence can easily be marred by an education which prevents him from developing his highest possibilities. Likewise, the free citizen will undoubtedly owe much to the formative influence of the society into which he is born. Although the influence of the government is a complex matter, as we shall see, it is clear from the very outset that if, as history abundantly shows, man can be made unhappy and wicked through inept or evil institutions, he can perhaps be made virtuous and happy through good ones, so that the essential political problem can be stated thus: 'What is the nature of the government suited to form the most virtuous, the most enlightened, the wisest—in a word, the best, taking this word in its greatest sense—people?' (i. 404-5).

In order to create a form of government which preserves the citizen's freedom, and yet exerts a beneficial influence upon his actions, it is necessary to overcome a serious obstacle: the corruption of all sound principles by the pernicious influence of society. However hypothetical Rousseau's reconstruction of human history in the second *Discours* may have been, it was clearly intended to show that the historical process had involved a grievous error of judgement on man's part and that history was the story of enslavement and misery rather than of liberation and happiness; it is thus impossible to base an analysis of human nature on a study of its historical development. In the same way sound political principles cannot be determined by a merely historical examination of any actual government, whether past or present. This no doubt explains the sub-title of Rousseau's main political treatise, 'Principles of political right'. The interdependence of politics and morality already noted will mean that political discussions must deal with principles rather than facts—

with establishing criteria and norms rather than with determining the nature of any particular government. It is not a question of studying men's actual political attitudes but of examining the foundations of all legitimate governments and the nature of political obligation. In this respect, Rousseau insists upon the difference between his work and Montesquieu's. In the last book of *Émile* he declares that 'political right has yet to be born'; in spite of his great reputation Grotius is 'a mere child' in this respect and, 'what is more, a dishonest child', while Hobbes, so often unjustly vilified at Grotius's expense, is nothing but a 'sophist'. 'The only modern writer capable of creating this great and useless [sic] science would have been the illustrious Montesquieu. But he took care not to treat questions of political right; he contented himself with treating the positive right of established governments; and there is nothing in the world more different than these two studies' (iv. 836). 'We have to know what ought to be', affirms Rousseau, 'in order to make a proper judgement of what is' (iv. 836). This explains the abstract character of the *Contrat social*, which relies, as Rousseau puts it in the *Confessions,* on the 'sole force of reasoning' (i. 405 n.).

On the other hand, the *Contrat social* is not intended to be merely utopian in the sense of being completely divorced from reality. Unlike Plato, and many of his successors, Rousseau is not concerned with the delineation of an ideal government, a unique model which can be imitated by all the rest; he has no desire to construct a system which, he says, would simply be relegated to the 'land of day-dreams'. No doubt the elaboration of sound critical principles applicable to any legitimate government will eventually lead to a reappraisal of the existing order and a constructive effort to eliminate some of its more glaring defects, but the starting-point for an adequate analysis of political right must be the clarification of general principles which go beyond the limits of existing institutions. At the same time the political thinker has to reconcile his ideal with the nature of 'men as they are' and not as he would simply like them to be. From this point of view the beginning of the *Contrat social* gives a very clear indication of the way in which Rousseau seeks to combine idealistic and realistic, moral and psychological, elements. He intends to take 'men as they are' and 'the laws as they may be' and to combine what 'right permits' with what 'interest prescribes'; questions of justice and right have to be united with the requirements of interest and utility. This means that Rousseau proposes to start with human nature rather than with abstract principles. By 'men as they are', he does not mean the corrupt beings of contemporary society, but men as they are in their 'original' being. His view of politics thus accords with his attitude towards the development of the individual. If Rousseau assumes man to be capable of moral effort and rational choice, he also insists on the importance of his concern with self-preservation and happiness. At whatever level we consider human nature, it is necessary to accept the cardinal fact that man will be always concerned with his own interest. The point made so emphatically in *Émile* reappears also in the political writings and is the basis of Rousseau's political realism. Men cannot be expected to enter a society that does not bring them positive advantages: the citizens will always seek to follow the principle of self-preservation, and it will be useless to exhort them to seek the common good, if they are not first of all assured of their own security and material well-being. At the same time, the attainment of moral and rational maturity will take them beyond mere selfishness towards a nobler and more personal form of self-fulfilment which they will also come to see as an expression of their true interest. Yet, at whatever level the political problem is considered, it will always presuppose that questions of right remain inseparable from those of interest.

Clearly the interdependence of personal and social factors involves a radical transformation of the notion of interest and the 'nature' of which it forms part. Since the happiness and well-being of the individual are bound up with those of the community as a whole, it is not enough for him to heed the voice of nature and to follow the spontaneous impulse of natural goodness. His involvement with other people will require the exercise of reason and will as well as the capacity to attain a virtue which enables him to subordinate immediate personal desire to a higher social good. We have already seen how, in order to achieve virtue, the individual may have to 'denature' himself inasmuch as he will need to rise above selfish desire and be able to become 'master of himself'. As soon as the notion of virtue is given a social emphasis, the need to denature primitive impulses becomes still more urgent. Yet this denaturing process is also accompanied by the individual's realization of himself as a rational and moral being who is fulfilling all the higher possibilities of his nature. As soon as he follows order instead of impulse, his existence is given an expansion, elevation, and plenitude that are unknown to primitive man. 'His ideas are extended, his feelings ennobled and his whole soul elevated' (*CS*, I. 8). From being a 'stupid, limited animal', he becomes 'an intelligent being and a man'.

If the establishment of political society is closely connected with this radical transformation and development of human nature, it cannot achieve its aim without a frank acceptance of the problem which lies at the heart of all sound political philosophy—the source and control of supreme power. The essential difficulty is that, at every stage of human existence, force involves inequality in some form or other; nothing can change the essential fact that men are born with different capacities and aptitudes. In the state of nature physical inequality presents no problem, because men's isolated and dispersed condition prevents any serious conflict; all have to face one fundamental limitation, physical necessity, which constitutes a universal condition governing every effort at self-preservation; this involves a general and inescapable form of equality which overrides all individual differences. In society, where men are brought into close contact with one another, physical inequality, if left unchecked, would lead to a disastrous distinction between strong and weak and a state of tyranny and oppression; the majority of men would be the helpless victims of a small but powerful minority. Rousseau's criticism of contemporary society lays great stress on this particular point. Some means, therefore, must be found of eliminating inequality, or, at least, of relating it to conditions which neutralize its harmful effects and divert it into politically useful channels.

Rousseau's solution is to bring together these various individual powers in a way which gives them collective expression and transforms them into a 'common force' aimed at the preservation and well-being of the community. Instead of allowing the power of each individual to compete with that of the rest, it is essential 'to find a form of association that defends and protects with *all the common force* the person and goods of *each* associate' (*CS*, I, 6). If every individual, whatever his particular strength, feels that he is being protected by the whole common force, then he will have no reason to fear oppression and injustice, for no other citizen or group of citizens will enjoy privileges which are denied to him; he will willingly give up the independent use of his own limited powers in order to enjoy the security and protection afforded by the total strength of the community acting as a single body.

This common force cannot be effective unless it involves all the citizens without exception. If the individual wishes to be protected by the united strength of the whole community, he, in his turn, must be prepared to make a complete surrender of his own power. 'Each of us puts his person and his entire power under the supreme direction of the general will; as a body, we receive each member as an indivisible part of the whole' (*CS*, I. 6). Rousseau insists that this unconditional 'alienation' is an indispensable condition for the survival of a valid political community. (Indeed, its practical expression, as we shall see, is much more limited, but at this stage, it is a question of defining right rather than fact.) This step enables the harmful effects of natural inequality to be offset by a new form of civil equality. In Rousseau's view, without this civil or conventional equality, no proper political freedom is possible, because the citizens will be constantly exposed to the threat of oppression.

The need to protect the State against the usurpation of power by particular individuals or groups is one of the overriding concerns of Rousseau's political philosophy. His desire to bind the individual indissolubly to the community is due largely to his distrust of the powerful who, in his opinion, always try to manipulate society for their own advantage. He puts the point very forcibly in a note to *Émile*: 'The universal spirit of the laws of every country is always to favour the strong against the weak, and the one who has against the one who has nothing: this drawback is inevitable and is without exception' (iv. 524 n.). In a more general way, however, Rousseau's insistence on the need to determine the ultimate source of political authority in a completely unambiguous way is one of the original features of his political outlook—certainly more significant than his use of the traditional idea of the 'social contract'. Accepting, in this respect, the emphasis of Hobbes's political views, Rousseau considers that no valid political philosophy is possible until the nature and origin of political sovereignty have been firmly and clearly established.

Because sovereignty is the ultimate source of authority, it must be absolute. This does not mean that it is arbitrary, but simply that it cannot be limited by anything other than itself. Although, as we shall see, its activity is to some extent restricted by its own intrinsic character, it cannot be dependent on any other political authority. In this respect sovereignty is to the State what *amour de soi* is to the individual—the indispensable instrument of its preservation. Sovereignty, however, is a collective, not a particular, form of *amour de soi*; the meaning of self-preservation in this case is determined by the nature of the political association, not by that of the individuals considered in isolation. No doubt the State, being made up of individuals, must consider their interest, but that interest has to be defined in a genuinely social, not a merely selfish, way. In other words, if the individual makes certain demands upon the association, in so far as he expects it to bring him security and well-being, he must also be prepared to accept his own share of responsibility. While acknowledging that the State is governed by the same fundamental principle as the one operating in his own life (self-preservation), he has to realize that the preservation of the State depends on the conditions and principles which have brought it into being as a voluntary civil association. To ensure its survival, the community as a whole must assume sole responsibility for the control of supreme power. This means that sovereignty cannot be bound by past decisions or promises for the future, for this would take absolute authority out of the citizens' hands and threaten the very basis of the political association. It would be absurd for the sovereign to 'give itself chains in the future' (*CS*, II. 1). 'It is against the nature of the body politic that the sovereign should impose upon itself a law which it cannot infringe' (*CS*, I. 7); 'the very moment there is a master, there is no longer a sovereign and the body politic is destroyed.'

The absolute character of sovereignty is not to be feared, because *amour de soi*, whether collective or particular, will never deliberately harm itself. 'The supreme power needs no guarantee towards its subjects,' affirms Rousseau, 'because it is impossible for the sovereign body to want to harm all its members' (*CS*, I. 7). This is a rule to which, says Rousseau, there is no exception: it would be illogical to expect the State to act against its own true interest. A further reason for accepting the absolute quality of sovereignty is the fact that *amour de soi*, being the authentic basis of all human existence, must be good in its essence. The natural goodness of man will manifest itself at every level, whether individual or social, as soon as conditions are propitious. The reciprocal obligation existing between the citizen and the political body ensures that its activity will always be right; 'the sovereign, by the very fact that it is, is always all that it should be' (*CS*, I. 7). 'Each one appropriates to himself this word "each"'; as a part of the sovereign power, the citizen knows that 'he cannot work for others without working for himself'. The concept of sovereignty is rooted in 'the preference which each gives himself and, consequently, in the nature of man' (*CS*. II. 4). The very interest which is at the basis of sovereignty will keep it loyal to its own intrinsic nature. Although sovereignty is not limited by any external authority, it must obviously obey the laws of its own being and respect the purpose for which it has been instituted; Rousseau, therefore, is justified in speaking of the 'limits' of this supreme power.

Since sovereignty is bound up with the community as a whole, it follows that it must be indivisible as well as absolute. In other words, defined as the supreme power or common force invested in the whole body of citizens, sovereignty cannot be less than itself. Any attempt to split off a part of it from the rest would destroy its essential character and change it from sovereignty to the mere power of the majority; because it belongs to all the citizens without exception, sovereignty has to be indivisible. Moreover, if it is indivisible, it is also inalienable, for the citizens cannot divest themselves of it without destroying the very basis of their existence as a political association. On this fundamental point Rousseau differs from Hobbes who had allowed sovereignty to be transferred to an all-powerful ruler. In Rousseau's view, the citizens can never transfer their supreme power or authority to anybody else. (This does not preclude, as we shall see, the possibility and even the necessity of delegating certain 'functions'.) Since sovereignty comes into existence with the foundation of the civil association, it can disappear only with the dissolution of that association and the return of the individuals who comprise it to the 'state of nature'.

Rousseau's conception of the political association rests upon a close interdependence of part and whole and it is noteworthy how frequently the terms 'each' and 'all' appear together in the discussion of sovereignty in the *Contrat social*. This is already apparent in Rousseau's enunciation of the fundamental problem of political association: 'To find a form of association which defends and protects the person and goods of each association with the entire common force, and through which each, uniting with all, yet obeys himself and remains as free as before' (I. 6). The same emphasis recurs later on when he affirms that 'each giving himself to all gives himself to nobody'.

Rousseau's conception of sovereignty establishes this link between 'each' and 'all' by presupposing a complete reciprocity and equality of commitment. The social pact, based on the idea of unanimous consent and absolute sovereignty, 'establishes among citizens such equality that they all commit themselves on the same conditions and must all enjoy the same rights'. Obligations and benefits must be an integral part of the citizens' life. To allow any individual to be exempt from either of these fundamental aspects of the civil association would make genuine political freedom impossible, because it would expose the citizens to one of the greatest threats to political justice—the inequality which arises from man's subjection to the arbitrary will of others.

Rousseau believes that men do not resent or fear dependence as such, but only an irrational and fortuitous dependence on other people. In *Émile* he had already put this point very forcibly:

There are two kinds of dependence: dependence on things, which belongs to nature; dependence on men, which belongs to society. Dependence on things, having no morality, is not harmful to freedom and does not engender vices; dependence on men, being uncontrolled, engenders them all, and it is through this dependence that master and slave become mutually depraved. If there is some means of curing this evil in society, it is through substituting law for man and arming the general will with a real strength that is superior to the influence of any particular will. If the laws of nations could have, like those of nature, an inflexibility which no human force could overcome, dependence on men would again become dependence on things: in the commonwealth all the advantages of the natural state would be combined with those of the civil state; to the freedom which keeps man exempt from vice would be added the morality which lifts him up to virtue (iv. 311).

The absolute, indivisible, and inalienable nature of sovereignty makes it possible to achieve this impersonal dependence—this dependence on things which avoids dependence on people by locating supreme political authority in all the members of the community. The conditions are equal for all, because all freely accept them; in obeying the common authority established by their own will, the citizens are in some sense obeying themselves. Indeed, they must obey themselves because there is no other power they *can* obey. Each citizen accepts this condition in the knowledge that it is accepted by all the rest: anything he is asked to do can also be demanded, if necessary, of his fellow citizens. Being inconceivable without genuine equality of right and obligation, sovereignty becomes the guarantor of freedom.

When sovereignty is understood in this manner, it does not take the form of mere power as such; its collective and social implications give it a particular quality which prevents it from being arbitrary and capricious. Just as the life of the individual is transformed by his participation in a society which makes him a free and intelligent being, so does the concept of sovereignty transform power by associating it with right. Since sovereignty does not exist as a simple physical fact, but as a force constituted and organized for a certain social purpose, it is bound to embody the characteristics of the act of will that has brought it into being. Moreover, since the citizens constitute a 'moral body', the moral element must be expressed through their collective strength. Sovereignty, therefore, is not a merely static concept, but is inseparable from the activity of will. (It is worth noting, in this respect, that sovereignty is linked up with Rousseau's wider view of morality as involving relationships: a physical entity acquires moral significance only through its active relation with other beings.)

The will which animates sovereignty is necessarily different from the particular will of an individual concerned with the satisfaction of his own desires; sovereignty involves a 'general will' inspired by social obligation rather than by selfish interest. In the first version of the *Contrat social* Rousseau had reproduced with approval Diderot's view of the general will as 'in each individual a pure act of the understanding which reasons, in the silence of the passions, concerning what man can demand of his fellow and what his fellow can demand of him' (iii. 286). Although Rousseau's notion of general will differs from Diderot's in as much as it involves only the citizen and not the individual as a member of the human race, it still has the same moral rectitude, the same need to subordinate selfishness to a general principle based on the common good. To become effective, therefore, sovereignty must be expressed as 'general will'. It is perhaps rather strange that Rousseau does not devote more space to the definition of this fundamental concept, one of the most important of his entire political philosophy. His comments, however, make it clear that the general will is intended to establish a qualitative distinction between two different attitudes—the responsible social attitude of the citizen concerned with the common good and the particular will of the individual who seeks merely his own advantage. Undoubtedly there is a deeper sense in which the citizen also seeks his 'interest', but he relates it to the preservation and well-being of the community as a whole rather than to the pursuit of his own petty advantage.

Rousseau carefully distinguishes the 'general will' from the 'will of all'; the latter is simply the physical sum of the particular desires of individuals who happen to be seeking the same objective. The mere coincidence of votes is no guarantee of rectitude: the fact that these different wills happen to form a majority vote—or even, in exceptional cases, a unanimous vote—in no way affects the basic attitude involved, for the 'will of all' may be nothing but the fortuitous expression of selfish desires which are harmful to the true interest of the State. The general will, on the other hand, presupposes a deliberate attitude of mind and a firm determination to seek the common good. As such, it is not susceptible to the vagaries, hesitations, and weaknesses which influence the behaviour of individuals, for, in Rousseau's words, the general will is always 'constant, incorruptible, and pure'. When it becomes less than this, it ceases to be the general will.

Why, then, does Rousseau insist, in a phrase which has perturbed liberal thinkers, that, in certain circumstances, the citizen may be 'forced to be free'? One of the reasons for this qualification is to be found in Rousseau's view of the political association. Like the individual, the body politic has its own personality, its particular self. It is 'a moral collective body', with 'its own unity, common ego, life and will' (I. 6). At the same time, the State is not a single homogeneous entity, but, like the individual, an entity containing different elements of which the will is only one. Just as the individual has also to reckon with the force of feeling and passion, so must the State take into account the pressure of particular influences which may sometimes conflict with the general will. No citizen is merely a citizen and nothing else; he is also an individual with his own desires and feelings which may sometimes be powerful enough to tempt him to subordinate his will as a citizen to his will as an individual, and so to seek his own advantage at the expense of the general good. Like the wicked man, he may seek to invert the order of things for his own interest, adapting the world to his particular needs rather than his own desires to those of the community. This does not mean that he is essentially bad or that his will has been irremediably corrupted, but simply that he has succumbed to weakness and has failed to recognize his own true interest; the activity of his will has been perverted by his erroneous judgement. In other words, although the citizen may always *will* his true interest, he may not always *see* it. The wayward citizen, therefore, may have to be reminded of his true interest, perhaps in spite of himself; he may have to be kept loyal—against his immediate wishes—to the principles of the civil association to which he has already given his free consent and which represent the expression of his own will as citizen. In this he will eventually be made aware of his need to respect the nature of his obligation to the community and, consequently, he will come to realize that he is obeying his own better self; in acquiescing in the common good rather than in his own selfish advantage, he will perceive that this is what, deep within him, he really wants to do.

These general principles lead to considerable practical difficulties, but they are quite consistent with Rousseau's basic conception of political authority. He admits that the only feasible expression of political opinion is the vote and that the community must usually be dependent on the majority vote, but he is anxious to point out that the vote as such is a purely physical activity which, of itself, has no moral value. For the same reason, a small virtuous minority may be closer to the general will than a large but misguided majority seeking some material advantage at the expense of the State's real interest. It is always the quality of the decision, not the outward expression, which determines its value; something more valid than a mere counting of votes is required if the citizens are to be sure that their decision is right. In practice, however, the vote is the citizens' only way of giving physical expression to their decisions.

In any case, the general will alone is not enough to secure the effective expression of its deeper social purpose. Just as the individual will has to be expressed through the personality as a whole, so does the general will require some kind of concrete and objective form if it is not to remain a merely abstract and empty intention. This is why it has to be embodied in the 'law'. Rousseau insists that the definition of the law need not become involved in metaphysical discussions about the 'law of nature (*CS*, II. 6). Although, as we shall see, there is a sense in which all political questions must ultimately relate to natural right, because they are inseparable from freedom, it is not necessary to relate the law (as does Montesquieu) to the 'nature of things'. Created by a deliberate act of will, the laws derive their meaning from the activity and situation which bring them into being. For this very reason they constitute the heart of the political community and are its life-principle. The laws are the 'driving force' of the body politic which is given 'activity and feeling only through them'; without the laws the State would be 'like a body without a soul'; they alone make it possible to achieve the 'prodigious feat' of persuading men to subordinate their own will to the common good. It is to the 'celestial voice' of the law that men owe justice and freedom.[2] When the laws are ignored or corrupted, the State is lost beyond redemption.

The supreme importance of the laws prevents Rousseau from considering them in any narrow legalistic sense. Their strength does not lie in their subtlety and complexity, but in their fewness and simplicity. The worst nation, he declares, is the one which has the most laws; the existence of numerous laws means that the citizens feel the need to subject themselves to external restraints instead of relying on their own inner strength. The real source of the laws is in men's hearts. When he attempts to draw up a constitution for Poland, Rousseau frequently insists on this point—that the only laws which will really benefit the Poles are those which they accept in the depth of their own being. The true sanctuary of the State is in the hearts of the Poles (Cf. iii. 1013, 1019). The 'citizens' heart', Rousseau writes in a fragment, 'is the State's best protection' (iii. 486). When there are few laws, the citizens' obedience depends on their own determination and loyalty rather than on the deterrent effect of an elaborate legal code.

The crucial role of the law involves Rousseau in a difficulty. Since the law has a solemn, almost sacred function as the factor responsible for shaping the nation's inner life, 'gods would be necessary to give laws to men'. The establishment of fundamental laws will clearly determine the entire history of the community. How, then, are they to be introduced? It is not a question of casting doubt upon man's essential goodness, but of bringing enlightenment to those who may be incapable of finding it by their own efforts. 'The general will is always right, but the judgement guiding it is not always enlightened' (*CS*, II. 6). People often need a guide to enable them to combine understanding and will in a way that contributes to their own well-being and that of the community as a whole. This no doubt explains Rousseau's preoccupation with the Lawgiver, the superior being who creates the principal laws of the State and is, therefore, the originator of the State itself. The true Lawgiver is Moses, the founder of the Jewish nation, or Numa, the founder of the Roman Republic, or Lycurgus, the founder of the Spartan constitution; such men had the responsibility of 'changing, so to speak, human nature' and of transforming isolated individuals into moral and social beings. It is the Lawgiver who is mainly responsible for effecting the radical transformation and 'denaturation' presupposed by man's participation in the civil association.

The Lawgiver is an interesting example of Rousseau's somewhat ambiguous attitude towards the problem of authority. Although his political principles are clearly democratic in their implications, in as much as they rest upon the notion of popular consent and sovereignty, he tends to doubt man's ability to put them into operation without the help of some kind of superior being. The same idea is apparent in the relationship between Émile and the tutor: Émile is to follow 'nature' and yet needs a guide to show him the way. The Lawgiver also has an educative function, for he is dealing with people who, politically speaking, are little more than children. On the other hand, he is never granted any official authority: he must persuade, not coerce; his real power lies always in 'his own great soul' and in the exercise of his 'sublime reason'. His function is to develop possibilities which already exist in the community but have not yet been fulfilled; he helps the people to see more clearly into their own character, but he cannot relieve them of the responsibility of deciding their own future.

These principles—the social contract, general will, sovereignty, and law—provide the basis of all valid constitutions, whatever their particular form. It was an important innovation on Rousseau's part that he deliberately excluded the notion of government from these general notions. Unlike some predecessors, he refused to allow any kind of contractual relationship between sovereign and government. Pufendorf, for example, had maintained that there were two con-tracts—the contract establishing the civil association and the 'contract or pact of submission' through which the citizens then handed over some of their power to the government or ruler. Rousseau emphati-cally rejected this idea. In his view, there can only be one contract: the one through which all the citizens, of their own free will, set up the civil association. The citizens never give up their legislative power. The members of the government or rulers are no more than the 'officers' or 'commissioners' charged by the people to perform certain tasks and functions; they are always accountable for their actions and can be removed from office whenever the people see fit. The government, therefore, has a very subordinate role, for its main function is to carry out the orders of the general will; having no power to initiate laws, it exists solely as the executive instrument of the sovereign will. In Rousseau's words, the government is merely the force or physical component of the State, while the sovereign is its heart and will. The executive body ultimately depends on the general will and sovereignty of which it is only an 'emanation'; it has no existence of its own right, but has only 'a borrowed or subordinate life' (*CS*, III. 1). Just as the human body cannot function without the soul, so does the government have to be sustained by the moral strength of the general will.

Although Rousseau is clearly opposed to any idea of a complete 'separation of powers' in Montesquieu's sense (for there is only one supreme power, the sovereign, which is absolute, indivisible, and inalienable), he insists that the government must have its own distinctive function. At first sight, perhaps, it might seem that the sovereign and government ought to be united, for then the 'body' would be directly carrying out the wishes of the 'soul', but this is neither wise nor feasible in practice. If the sovereign were to take over the executive, as well as the legislative, function and so become involved with carrying out its own laws, it would run the grave risk of forgetting its concern with the common good. It is important for the sovereign not to become absorbed in particular activities, but to be able to inspect the government, to survey it at a certain distance and to watch the way in which the general laws are being carried out; any involvement with particular acts would probably weaken the effectiveness of its legislative will.

The relations of sovereignty and government are bound up with the different functions exercised by the members of the political association. The 'people' as a whole can always be considered from two points of view: as sovereign, they have a clearly defined role in initiating legislation; as the 'State', however, they are also 'subjects' who merely obey the laws for which they are responsible as sovereign. The government serves as an intermediary between these two functions. In Rousseau's phraseology, the government exists 'between the whole and the whole', that is, the people considered as a whole, and yet from two distinct points of view—sovereign and subjects. The government facilitates communication between the two functions by transmitting the people's own orders as 'sovereign' to itself as 'subjects'.

With his discussion of government, Rousseau leaves the domain of absolute principles for a consideration of the relative factors which play an important part in political life. Although he does not adopt a purely empirical standpoint, he makes an elaborate attempt to work out a 'science of government': on the basis of a mathematical proportion, he tries to determine the changing relationship between 'sovereign', 'government', and 'subjects'; a sound State involves a varying series of checks and balances adjusted to the changes in the strength of three particular constituents. The size of a government, for example, will depend on that of the territory and the number of citizens. It is not necessary to follow Rousseau in these complicated and somewhat unrewarding pages of the *Contrat social*, but his argument makes it clear that he is fully aware of the relativist aspects of political theory. When discussing the Lawgiver, he already insists upon the need to take into account the particular characteristics of the nation that is to be founded; the political structure of any community depends on many factors—the size of the territory and population, the fertility of the soil, as well as particular habits and customs.

These considerations are especially important in any discussion of the nature of 'government'. In general, Rousseau uses the term 'democracy' in the ancient sense to mean a government by the people acting as a body and exercising both legislative and executive functions; this kind of democracy is obviously different from the modern idea of representative government. On the whole, he thinks this form of government is impracticable, being suited only to a very small State and to a people of 'gods' or beings capable of a superhuman control of their passions and feelings. He considers aristocracy to be the most sensible form of government, since its essential moderation makes it suitable for States of medium size and power. Of monarchy, Rousseau has some harsh things to say, since he believes that 'kings want to be absolute' (*CS*, III. 6): they will always seek the maintenance of their own power at the expense of their subjects. Even so, with all its limitations, monarchy appears to be the only form of government suited to large States. In Rousseau's opinion, however, little can be done to help such States, for he considers them to be already on the road to perdition.

Although Rousseau believes it possible to work out a formula for the best kind of government appropriate to each state, he does not believe that there is a single model which can be copied by all. There is a government which is best for one particular nation, but which, by that very fact, would be unsuited to the rest (*CS*, III. viii). Respect for general principles must also take into account the needs of particular situations. When he is trying to draw up a constitution for Poland, he is careful to insist on the importance of respecting the distinctive 'genius, character, and tastes of the nation' (iii. 960). Nothing could be more disastrous than to follow the example of an age that had let genuine individuality be replaced by anonymous uniformity; instead of there being distinct nations in the modern world, we find only featureless Europeans with the same unvarying feelings and habits. His own principles, on the other hand, allow him to admit that 'the foundations of the State are the same in every government', and to recognize at the same time that each form of government has 'its own reason which makes it preferable to any other, according to men, times and places' (iii. 811).

More original than Rousseau's analysis of the mechanics of government is his discussion of political attitudes and their relationship with society as a whole. He frankly acknowledges the powerful influence of passion and feeling upon political loyalty and, to some extent, this explains the strain of pessimism running through his political thought: he knows that selfish interest is always likely to militate against any kind of idealism. 'The law of the strongest', though incompatible with 'right', is an inescapable element of human life, especially in society, and, as we have seen, Rousseau believes that the powerful will always use the laws to secure their own advantage at the expense of the weak. The political idealist is thus faced with a formidable problem: how is it possible to persuade men to put the law above themselves? The problem is as difficult as the mathematical one of 'squaring the circle' and, in his most pessimistic moments, Rousseau sees no alternative between 'the most austere democracy' or 'the most complete Hobbism', the former being an unattainable ideal, the latter naked absolutism.[3] The principle of power will always tend to encroach on the influence of right. Interest, the vital principle of every existence, though capable of moral and spiritual expression, too often tends to become 'self-interest' in a degraded materialistic or psychological sense.

If Rousseau makes extensive use of mathematical and mechanistic analogies to describe his science of government, he makes even wider use of biological images to describe the life and death of the State. It is impossible, he says, to legislate for eternity, for even the finest constitutions are doomed to perish, and the principle of decay and corruption ultimately destroys every State. The body politic, he declares, begins to die from the very moment of its birth and bears within itself the causes of its own destruction. Men can do no more than delay this process. Nevertheless, the situation is not hopeless. Although States, like human beings, have varying degrees of robustness, there is an important difference between the human constitution and the body politic: whereas the former is the work of nature, the latter is the work of art. If man cannot prolong his own life, he can prolong that of the State by careful thought, and especially by developing a sound political attitude which keeps disruptive forces in check.

Rousseau's firm conviction that power groups will constantly tend to seek satisfaction at the expense of the community explains many particular aspects of the *Contrat social*. Realizing that every member of the government will always be an individual with a particular will as well as an official with a corporate will, Rousseau stresses the tendency of rulers and officials to let their personal desires dominate their sense of civic responsibility. He tries to counteract this danger by maintaining and strengthening the unity of the political association. This preoccupation with unity is one of the most characteristic features of his political outlook and has far-reaching effects upon his conception of the ideal community. He seeks to make the citizen dependent on the State in a way that not only frees him from dependence on others, but also prevents him from associating with them for some anti-social purpose.

Although Rousseau admits that no single State can serve as a model for all the rest, he believes that certain kinds of society are far preferable to others. In this respect he looks back to the past rather than forward to the future. His criticism of large towns makes it clear that he would have viewed with abhorrence the emergence of modern industrial states with their vast urban populations. His own preference was for the old Greek city-state and the early Roman republic. Sparta, for example, is constantly praised as the epitome of a compact community based on a strong civic sense. Nearer his own time he considered the Swiss to have retained many of the praiseworthy characteristics of ancient institutions in the face of the ever-encroaching corruption of the modern world. Although the *Contrat social* was not modelled on Geneva, Rousseau was probably justified in claiming that it was 'written for Geneva and small States like it' (i. 935), because it was only in them that his ideas could ever hope to find adequate expression. Although he may not have had a very adequate conception of the real Geneva but tended to see it through the idealizing activity of his imagination, his native republic probably had a certain influence upon the formulation of his political ideas and encouraged his predilection for the small, closely-knit community.

Rousseau did not admire such States solely for their compactness and unity, but also for the way in which they were able to express the genuinely human aspects of civic life. At times the strongly abstract form of the *Contrat social* makes Rousseau's political principles seem somewhat remote from everyday reality, but his projected constitutions for Corsica and Poland show a curious fusion of idealism and realism. Although he never visited Poland, he carefully studied the documents and material supplied to him by Count Wielhorski, as well as the projected reforms already suggested by Mably. At the same time, the Poland that took shape in his mind became a country expressing many of his own favourite political ideas. Since Poland was a large State, Rousseau sought to make it amenable to his principles by giving it a federal form, so that it would no longer be a cumbersome entity but a federation of small units held together by a common purpose. The Corsica of the *Projet* is an even more personal evocation; although Rousseau again makes an effort to base his suggestions on the information supplied to him by the Corsican leaders, he clearly incorporates into the projected constitution many of his own dreams and aspirations.

In both these works he acknowledges that political loyalty cannot be based on the acceptance of merely abstract principles, however valid they may be in themselves, but must be found in the hearts of the citizens. The most effective way of expressing such feelings is to imbue the citizens' sense of national solidarity with the fervour and enthusiasm of genuine patriotism. This is a theme which runs right through Rousseau's writings, for in the very first *Discours* he deplores the way in which modern man 'smiles disdainfully at these old words "religion" and "patriotism" '. One of his first political writings, the *Encyclopédie* article 'Économie politique', also gives a prominent place to patriotism, affirming that the

greatest prodigies of virtue have been produced by love of the father-land—this sweet and lively feeling which joins the force of pride to all the beauty of virtue, gives it an energy which, without disfiguring it, makes it the most heroic of all passions. It is patriotism which produced so many immortal actions whose brilliance dazzles our weak eyes, and so many great men whose virtues are considered to be mere fables since love of the fatherland has been turned to derision. (iii. 255)

Clearly Rousseau's conception of patriotism is not the same as modern nationalism, for it takes the form of 'patriotic intoxication' and 'heroic zeal'; it contains a profound moral inspiration and an indissoluble link with virtue and freedom. National feeling is not valid for its own sake, but solely for its human and civic content. At the same time, Rousseau admits that man's feelings cannot be easily extended to embrace the whole human race; the love of humanity as such, though a noble ideal, cannot provide an adequate basis for civil loyalty, for the 'feeling of humanity evaporates and weakens as it is extended over the whole earth' (iii. 254). Men will never be as sensitive to the misfortunes of remote peoples as they are to those of their fellow countrymen. Only patriotism can provide the powerful and intense feeling which provides a solid basis for national life.

Yet because patriotism is a complex attitude, the wise ruler will be careful to stimulate its psychological elements. In the *Contrat social* and elsewhere Rousseau insists that people are more readily swayed by opinion than by reason. The Legislator, for example, will pay particular attention to 'manners, customs, and especially opinion', for without these no political success will be possible (iii. 394). 'Whoever undertakes to found a nation', he declares, 'must know how to dominate opinions and, through them, govern men's passions' (iii. 965-6). Opinion is the unwritten law which, being 'engraved in the hearts of the citizens', is much more important than the effect of legal codes. In the long run habit is more powerful than authority in determining political and social attitudes, for people will more readily obey their own impulses than the orders of others.

Yet mere feeling, however socially beneficial, cannot serve as the sole basis of national life; it needs to be strengthened by a more powerful and stable element. True patriotism is not a simple emotion, but includes 'vigour of soul'—a firm moral attitude capable of overcoming all crises. It is probably this overriding concern with the need for moral strength that explains Rousseau's late introduction of the subject of 'civil religion' into a work which at first sight seemed to be restricted to a purely secular treatment of political theory. Rousseau perhaps realized that mere rational assent to sound principles and the more tenuous psychological acceptance of patriotic and other feelings might not be effective enough to secure the citizen's wholehearted loyalty. The idea of civil religion is introduced as a radical, even desperate, attempt to provide the State with an ultimate sanction capable of putting the law above men. Although Rousseau probably did not at first intend to use it in the *Contrat social*, it was certainly not new, for he had already discussed the idea of a 'civil profession of faith' in the 1756 letter to Voltaire on Providence. As we have seen, he believed that love of humanity was too vague and weak an emotion to be completely compatible with the citizen's wholehearted devotion to his country, while traditional religious beliefs, being based on the idea of special 'revelation', engendered bigotry, fanaticism, and internal discord. Civil religion was thus an attempt to adapt the basic principles of natural religion to civil life. Its 'few and simple' doctrines, declared Rousseau, were to be 'enunciated with precision, without explanation or commentary': 'the existence of a powerful, intelligent, beneficent, foreseeing, and provident divinity, the future life, the happiness of the just, the punishment of the wicked, the sacredness of the social contract and the laws' (iii. 468). There was to be one negative dogma: the exclusion of all intolerance. Such doctrines are not, truly speaking, religious dogmas, but *sentiments de sociabilité* without which it is impossible to be either 'a good citizen or a faithful subject'. What has shocked so many later thinkers is the strange condition which Rousseau attaches to this civil religion. Although nobody can be obliged to accept it, any one who refuses to do so will be banished from the State, not because he is 'impious', but because he is 'anti-social' (*insociable*), that is, incapable of putting the call of duty above his own selfish desires. Without in any way trying to justify Rousseau's attitude, we may point out that, in his view, the principles of civil religion were so solid and clear that no rational being ought to reject them; anyone who did so was either a madman or a criminal and so unfitted to be a member of society. Moreover, even a liberal thinker like Locke did not hesitate to exclude atheists from his State. Although Rousseau's ideas were certainly incompatible with the more genuinely progressive views of the *philosophes* on religious toleration, they were not uncommon in his day.

There seems to be no adequate reason for supposing that Rousseau's political ideas are in any way inconsistent with the principles developed in his other didactic writings. It may be useful, however, to indicate briefly their relationship with the views of earlier thinkers, whether of the liberal tradition or the school of Natural Law. Particularly important is the connection between his view of freedom and the outlook of his predecessors. In spite of the severe criticism to which Rousseau's view of freedom has been subjected—and in its most extreme form this criticism makes him a forerunner of totalitarianism rather than liberalism—there seems little justification for doubting the sincerity of his view of himself as a defender of freedom, whether or not he was mistaken about the practical implications of his ideas.

In spite of significant differences of approach to the problem, Rousseau and Locke are at one in their common emphasis upon the importance of freedom. Both thinkers believe that a political association is brought into existence by a voluntary act on the part of its participants and that a freely agreed contract is its only legitimate basis. Society does not simply emerge from a previous state, nor can it be created by force; it originates in a deliberate decision. This is why both Locke and Rousseau insist on the traditional idea of a social contract made between equals and not between rulers and subjects. The concept of political society is inseparable from the fact that men are, in Locke's phrase, 'naturally free'.

This close agreement on a fundamental aspect of political theory does not preclude an important divergence of outlook when they come to an analysis of the 'state of nature'. Like the thinkers of the Natural Law School, Locke believes that men in the state of nature are not only 'free and equal', but already familiar with certain rights, such as 'life, health, liberty, and possessions', and with the moral obligation that 'no one ought to harm another' in the exercise of these rights; the transition from nature to society does not involve any radical alteration to man's being, for 'the law of nature' operates in both conditions. In the state of nature, it is true, man has to rely mainly on his own strength, but even then he is potentially a rational and social being already aware of the limits of his power and of his need for other people; the main drawback to the primitive condition is that natural rights are insecurely held and that there is no common judge to settle disputes. Men enter society, therefore, to place their natural rights under the protection of the community as a whole. This means that the State's function remains a predominantly protective one, being carefully restricted to the protection of rights relevant to man's social conduct. Basically, Locke's freedom is 'freedom from external restraint' and presupposes a society that treats all its members as equals and respects the inviolability of their private rights.

For Rousseau, as we have seen, the function of the political association is far more creative than this, for it is only through his participation in society that man becomes truly rational and moral. Far from being a rational and social creature in the state of nature, he is essentially a creature of instinct, without moral sense or social feeling; it is only when he enters society that he acquires a moral outlook and a knowledge of right and wrong. 'Natural right' in the state of nature consists mainly of appetite and power. Rousseau is thus at one with Hobbes and Spinoza in accepting the essentially irrational, animal-like nature of primitive man; he constantly criticizes thinkers who read back into the nature of primitive man characteristics which derive from his membership of the social community. Whereas the natural state undergoes no change or progression, man's character is radically transformed as soon as he moves on to a new and higher stage of development. 'The isolated man always remains the same; he makes progress only in society'; it is only 'mutual frequentation' that makes possible the development of 'the most sublime faculties' (iii. 533, 477). Unlike many predecessors, Rousseau thus sees man's being in dynamic, rather than static terms; in the course of his development, the individual acquires capacities which were lacking or, at most, merely potential in his early condition.

Agreeing with Hobbes about the irrational nature of primitive man, Rousseau none the less vigorously repudiates his view of the state of nature as one of 'continual fear and danger of violent death' and as one in which each man, seeking to be 'foremost', is exposed to the aggressive behaviour of his fellow-men. Far from treating the life of man as 'solitary, poor, nasty, brutish, and short', Rousseau, as we have seen, considers his primitive condition to have been happy and peaceful; man eventually left it because of the pressure of external circumstances, not through his own free choice. Hobbes, on the other hand, treats the establishment of society as man's rational attempt to find the 'peace, security, and happiness' which he cannot obtain in his natural state. Morality and right thus come into existence with the founding of the civil association; but, unlike Rousseau, Hobbes apparently does not believe that man's inner nature is capable of any significant change: inwardly he remains just as selfish and aggressive as before. Henceforth, however, he is compelled to observe the law which is identified with the 'command of him that hath power'. Whether man is good or bad in himself does not matter as long as his behaviour accords with the principles of right and wrong embodied in the laws.

While placing, like Hobbes, great emphasis upon the notion of sovereignty as the ultimate, indivisible source of power, Rousseau refuses to draw Hobbes's absolutist conclusion. Whereas the English philosopher's pessimistic view of human nature causes the establishment of the civil association to be followed by the transfer of the citizens' rights to a supreme ruler, Rousseau holds fast to a strongly democratic view of sovereignty as the indivisible and inalienable right of the people; because of the rectitude of the general will, ultimate political authority may be safely left in the people's hands. Indeed, it would be folly, in Rousseau's opinion, to place it anywhere else. Moreover, justice is not a merely external principle imposed upon the people by some outside authority, but the authentic expression of its own moral autonomy. In this respect, Rousseau seems to be nearer to Spinoza than Hobbes, for although Spinoza believed that right was equated with power, he also insisted that society could help to make man a rational being capable of exercising a genuinely human freedom.

Are we then to suppose that Rousseau rejects 'natural right' as a political principle? He certainly criticizes traditional views of natural right, especially the one which already allows it to exist in the state of nature. In Rousseau's view, man comes to a full realization of his being only in the course of a long development. 'Natural right' itself must be gradually transformed and adapted to each stage of human growth; it is not an immutable, static principle always operating in the same way. It is important to distinguish between what Rousseau calls 'natural right properly speaking' (the primitive right of the state of nature) and 'reasoned natural right' appropriate to the social state. Whereas the former is a vague feeling or a spontaneous impulse without any moral significance, the latter involves 'nature, habit, reason, and our willingness to act with other men as we would wish them to act with us'. Mere sensibility gives way to reason and will. Yet, in each case, it is a question of remaining faithful to the intrinsic qualities of man's being. *Amour de soi* and freedom manifest themselves at every stage of existence, but from being 'natural' and 'independent' at the primitive level, they assume a moral and rational form in society. Rousseau's political theory, therefore, like the rest of his ideas, is related to his general view of man as a free and intelligent being whose needs cannot be those of a creature of instinct and appetite. Civil and moral freedom are not the same as natural freedom, even though all forms of freedom are grounded in human existence. Political right differs from primitive right, because it results from an act of will and, in this sense, is something deliberately created by human action; yet it is not intended to violate man's true nature, for its main function is to help him to fulfil himself in all essential aspects of his being. Even political right cannot ride roughshod over basic human feelings. That is why Rousseau is so firmly opposed to the despotism which denies man's most fundamental attribute—his freedom.

A distinguishing feature of Rousseau's conception of political ideas is the close link established between freedom and law, both of these concepts being dependent on a certain view of human nature and its place in the world. Although men are free to work out their own destiny, their freedom can never lead to arbitrary behaviour. Only when he has become the member of an organized society will the individual be able to bring order into his life and achieve the virtue and moral freedom which make him master of himself. No doubt political society has ultimately to be seen within the wider context of the 'order of nature', which expresses itself both as the universal system embracing all forms of being and as principles which are 'engraved in the human heart in indelible characters'; political institutions seem to stand midway between the primitive conditions of the state of nature and the eternal order of the universe. They differ from both, however, in as much as the 'nature' they express is not some simple given fact, but a new nature created by a deliberate act of will. Whereas the state of nature is too far below authentic human nature, and God's universal system too far above it, to be affected by man's action, civil society is a distinctly human achievement, expressing all the authentic possibilities of a free being. Admittedly, political action, like all other forms of human experience, cannot remain unmindful of the principles expressed through the order of nature and the nature of man himself, but the continued existence of the body politic remains dependent on the human will. That is why any refusal to support the civil association by free consent will necessarily return man to the undisciplined and irrational condition of the state of nature.

Notes

1. Cf. *Contrat social* (quoted hereafter as *CS*), II. vi (iii. 378).
2. Cf. 'Économie politique', iii. 248.
3. Cf. *Political Writings* (ed. Vaughan), ii. 161.

8
Aesthetic Ideas

ALTHOUGH Rousseau never produced any systematic exposition of his aesthetic ideas, he acknowledged the importance of literary art, as well as of good taste, for he believed that the experience of beauty played an important part in the life of the mature individual. However, he was convinced that aesthetic principles, like those of philosophy, education, or political theory, could not be considered in isolation from the rest of the personality. This is already obvious from his observations about the corrupting influence of society upon all human values. In his opinion, art had inevitably suffered from the effects of this general degradation. We have already seen how Rousseau considers the theatre to be a typical example of modern decadence. Its defects go far beyond the limitations of any particular writer's genius; as the product of an artificial and corrupt civilization, it is tainted at its very source. The features of modern plays, as well as the character and outlook of the actors and their audience, express the false values of the environment which has produced them. Rousseau insists that the theatre always reflects the emotions and vices of the people it serves; it is the servant, never the arbiter, of public opinion. If geniuses like Racine and Molière have been unable to escape the pernicious influence of their environment (by making, as in *Bérénice*, an emperor hesitate to sacrifice his love to duty or, as in *Le Misan-*

thrope, a virtuous man the butt of ridicule,) how can the ordinary theatre hope to offer worthy lessons to men in need of moral improvement?

The rehabilitation of art is inseparable, in Rousseau's opinion, from that of human nature. Since he believes that true education involves the progressive unfolding of man's innate capacities, nature, while possessing many varied facets and containing a hierarchy of values, constitutes a harmonious unity which should be reflected in the life of the developing individual. The supreme satisfaction of the mature being will be found in his contemplation of the universal order of which he feels himself to form an essential part. As soon as he has become aware of the true origins of his being, he will realize that all his activities are rooted in the same fundamental values and serve the same moral purpose; it is only their mode of expression which varies according to time and circumstance. Since every human activity, including the experience of art, can eventually be traced back to the same creative source, beauty and goodness will differ only in their outward form. No doubt in the next life their close connection will become still more evident, for one of the good man's rewards will be to contemplate the 'beauty of order'. Rousseau constantly stresses the close link between aesthetic and moral qualities and their dependence on the idea of order. As *Émile* approaches maturity, he will find that 'the true principles of justice, the true models of beauty, all the moral relations of beings, all ideas of order, are engraved in his understanding' (iv. 548). The common source of all these activities is 'well-ordered nature' and its human counterpart is *amour de soi*, which, says Rousseau, is 'always good and in conformity with order' (iv. 491). This explains why our reaction to the sight of virtue and our admiration for truly heroic actions often seem to be similar to our experience of beauty, for 'a soul truly touched by the charms of virtue must be correspondingly sensitive to all other kinds of beauty' (ii. 59).

This interdependence of aesthetic and moral values cannot be explained by means of abstract words or intellectual concepts; the affinity of art and morality must be sought at a deeper level of personal experience—in the 'true affections of the soul' and the 'ordered progress of our primitive affections' (iv. 523). It is here that we shall find the 'enthusiasm' which is an essential constituent of both art and morality. Enthusiasm for virtue, in Rousseau's opinion, is not distinguishable from the love of beauty. In each case we are transporting ourselves beyond the confines of private interest in order to experience feelings of an expansive kind. This expansive movement is a sign that we are not satisfied with our own petty world, but are aware of our capacity for a higher kind of fulfilment; true enthusiasm is inseparable from the aspiration towards a spiritual ideal. The enthusiasm of art and morality thus reveals man's desire for perfection and his ability to develop the idealistic possibilities of his nature. At the same time, this enthusiastic aspiration towards perfection would be impossible without the existence of a spiritual order— a universal system grounded in the Creator of all true values (iv. 596; 743).

In spite of their common origin in enthusiasm, aesthetic and moral activities have their own distinctive features. Although the human personality forms an essential unity, it possesses various powers, not all of which are called into play at the same time. Where aesthetic and moral principles diverge is in the particular personal attitude required by the specific function of each. In the main, beauty involves an attitude of contemplation, whilst morality requires an active relationship with oneself and other people: man is a spectator of beauty, but a participant in moral conduct. No doubt that is why Saint-Preux can tell Julie that 'the good is only the beautiful in action, that the one is intimately connected with the other and that they both have a common source in well-ordered nature' (ii. 59). If goodness and beauty are both permeated by the same essential quality, they none the less express themselves in different ways. It is thus possible to adopt an aesthetic attitude towards morality, as, for example, when we simply admire the heroism of 'great souls' and allow ourselves to be moved by the beauty of their virtue; at other times we can treat artistic matters in a moral spirit, as does Rousseau himself when he considers the effects of the theatre upon our conduct.

Apart from this difference between contemplative and practical attitudes, there is also the important connection of aesthetic appreciation with sensibility. Although it is not possible to make a complete break between morality and sensibility, the affective element is particularly prominent in aesthetic experience and produces a typically contemplative attitude towards order, whereas the emotional aspect of morality has to be subordinated to the activity of the will, the exercise of freedom and the attainment of virtue. Any aesthetic element that may be present in our moral outlook does not constitute its distinctive quality, but simply shows that there is a point of contact between the two at the level of sensibility; whatever satisfaction we may obtain from the contemplation of moral conduct, the latter is still dependent on will rather than feeling. The contemplation of beauty, on the other hand, is associated with objects rather than people. Ultimately it must have a metaphysical basis, since it involves our reactions to the order of God's creation; the experience of beauty is impossible without the presence of 'well-ordered nature'.

If the contemplative aesthetic attitude is inspired by the beauty of the external world, its perfection and enthusiasm are due mainly to our perception of the world as an ordered unity rather than as a collection of isolated objects; the aesthetic response is elicited by the 'perfection of the whole machine' and the general impression derived from the 'harmony and accord of the whole'. 'True magnificence', declares Rousseau in *La Nouvelle Héloïse*, 'is only order made perceptible on a big scale'. The highest form of beauty is to be found in the contemplation of the universe as a whole. Admittedly, as finite beings, we cannot see the entire universal system, but obtain only brief glimpses of its grandeur, but Rousseau is convinced that one of the joys of the next life will be the contemplation of this ordered system in all its beauty and splendour.

The aesthetic attitude is not very different from the feeling for nature which, at its highest, contains the same idealistic and spiritual response to beauty, for the perception of order at every level of experience is ultimately inseparable from the contemplation of the divine power which has produced it. God has left his spiritual imprint on the physical objects he has created by establishing connections between them and relating the whole physical system to his own divine plan, so that the true meaning of material objects can be properly understood only when they are contemplated in their proper setting. If man is able to perceive the accord between the spiritual and physical aspects of the universe, it is because he knows that his

own physical body—like the material world itself—is but the outward
expression of spiritual values.

Although the aesthetic attitude is only one aspect of a deeper
metaphysical appreciation of the universal order, Rousseau admits
that it may be analysed in the light of its own particular characteristics. As long as we do not forget its ultimate dependence on the
original source of all experience, art can be considered as a distinctly
human activity. At this more restricted level, a useful distinction can
be made between 'taste' and creative 'art'. Although taste falls short
of great art, Rousseau insists that it is not to be despised; it may be
merely 'the art of knowing all about little things' (iv. 677), but little
things still have a definite place in life; man cannot live permanently
in a rarefied spiritual atmosphere. The chief difference between taste
and the highest forms of artistic activity is that the former operates
mainly at the sensuous or physical level, while the latter are more
closely tied to spiritual values. Taste originates in 'pure sensations'
and our relations to material objects. Yet even these sensations require
cultivation and development, so that true taste combines both sensibility and judgement. 'One learns to see as one learns to feel.' An
exquisite sight is only a delicate and fine feeling.' 'Taste', concludes
Rousseau, 'is in some way the microscope of judgement' (ii. 59), for it
puts small objects within the range of judgement. The senses have to
be trained to see, as the emotions have to be trained to feel. The
appreciation of virtue and beauty involves a process of education;
it is because of his more highly cultivated taste that the truly sensitive
painter will grow enthusiastic over objects to which the untrained eye
will remain indifferent.

Since the development of taste obviously owes a great deal to the
influence of the environment, its form will vary from one culture to
another. Perhaps this is why Rousseau defines taste in a rather vague
manner as 'the faculty of judging what pleases or displeases the
majority' and good taste as that of 'the greatest number' (iv. 671).
It is difficult to determine the proper objects of taste, because their
arbitrary and artificial character makes them remote from genuine
human needs. Since taste owes a great deal to imitation, it will tend
to be formed by such factors as climate, manners, and government,
as well as by age, sex, and character (iv. 672). This means that, al-

though taste is natural to all men, it exists in different degrees and is extremely variable. The extent of a man's taste is determined by his innate sensibility, while its particular form and mode of expression depend clearly on his environment. In order to be able to compare different objects of taste, it is necessary to have known many societies, including those which leave people with enough wealth and luxury to amuse themselves and yet prevent inequality from being great enough to let fashion stifle taste. In any case, Rousseau recognizes that the formation of taste will involve a combination of physical, psychological, and moral factors.

Hostile though he is to the influence of urban life, Rousseau admits that it is only in a large city like Paris that good taste can be effectively cultivated. However corrupt people may be, they cannot develop their ideas and taste without the co-operation of others; taste, like reflection, presupposes a capacity for making subtle distinctions and this capacity can be developed only in places where people think, read, and converse. More especially, taste is impossible without mature judgement which, in its turn, can be cultivated only in a large city; good taste is thus acquired in a place where there are actually many people with bad taste! Consequently, it is important to distinguish between acquiring the instrument of good taste and using it (as in corrupt societies) for unworthy ends; good taste presupposes an ability to distinguish between good and bad objects. All true models of taste, therefore, are not to be found in the artificial products of a corrupt society, but only in nature (iv. 672). The further we go from our true master, the more disfigured our pictures will be. Only objects which we love and feel to have a genuine affinity with our own essential being can become true models of taste. That is why, on the whole, the works of the ancients are preferable to those of the moderns; the latter may show greater intellectual refinement, but they have less vigour and are further from nature. The genius of the ancients is more truly their own, because it is inspired by nature itself.

Contemporary writers have become too sophisticated and subtle, and their works too superficial, for them to be able to understand the only worthy object of taste—nature. Although they have acquired a knowledge of the human heart that was unknown to the ancient world, this knowledge is far from beneficial in its effects, since it is often related to vice rather than to virtue. What a man learns about his fellows from the plays he sees in the theatre is likely to provide him with a pessimistic view of mankind! A psychologically and aesthetically interesting subject-matter may be morally blameworthy. (Even Rousseau himself was not free from a certain ambivalence in this matter, for he admitted that he was fascinated by the very theatre he attacked so vigorously.) In a corrupt society a man's taste may respond to objects of which his soul disapproves. Even so, Rousseau concedes that in such a situation it may be necessary to leave people with a pernicious form of amusement like the theatre, lest its removal should be followed by the appearance of still more terrible vices! If the ancients provide a healthy corrective to the decadence of contemporary taste, it is because their works reveal a 'certain simplicity of taste which goes to the heart' (iv. 475). Although it may be necessary to cultivate sensibility and intelligence, all educative efforts will be either useless or harmful if they are not based on the kind of natural feelings which we find in the ancients. True taste is inconceivable without the genuine purity and simplicity which make an immediate appeal to the inner life.

The corruption of contemporary taste is yet another indication of man's failure to realize that the development of one side of his personality ought not to be separated from the rest. In an absolute sense, therefore, Rousseau believes that a good writer must also be a good man. In the *Dialogues*, he makes repeated and desperate efforts to prove the innocence of his own character from the moral qualities of his writings; the strategy of his enemies, he believes, has been to cast doubts on the authorship of his works by trying to prove that a 'monster' like him could not have written the exalted works published under his name! This connection between taste and personal integrity is not surprising in view of Rousseau's constant insistence upon the need to relate taste to simple, natural feeling: 'good taste is related to good morals'.

However, to relate the 'nature' which should serve as the model of taste to the idea of simplicity and goodness is not to explain the creative aspect of artistic activity. We have so far been dealing with Rousseau's account of the aesthetic attitude and with the characteristics of the man of taste; it is now time to look briefly at the artist himself. As soon as he comes to consider creative art, Rousseau follows his contemporaries and predecessors in stressing the idea of imitation. The significance of his use of the principle of the 'imitation of nature' can be more clearly understood if we consider his view of the individual arts, and especially of the art in which he had a particular interest—music. In this respect, some of his observations in his *Dictionnaire de musique* are particularly valuable. Needless to say, Rousseau's confidence in the principle of imitation is strengthened by his acceptance of the order of nature, which provides the framework and subject-matter of the artist's activities, as it does the basis of good taste. Every man possesses a certain capacity for imitation which ought to be related, as we have seen, to the existence of well-ordered nature. In modern society, however, imitation, though prompted by a 'desire to transport oneself outside oneself,' is based on unworthy psychological motives—vanity or jealousy—and soon degenerates into vice. Most contemporary art, therefore, assumes a merely artificial, ephemeral, and corrupt form, for it imitates the objects supplied to it by the social environment: only the art which is grounded in nature can achieve a solid and durable expression.

In the first place, the artist has to draw his material from some aspect of the physical world; the painter uses colours and the musician sounds. Yet these physical components are not enough to provide the artist with all he needs and, in this respect, a further consideration of the principle of well-ordered nature will provide us with valuable help in our understanding of creative art. Just as the beauty of physical objects does not lie in their isolated existence, but in their relations with one another, so does the artist's material have to be organized in accordance with a principle capable of transforming it into an object of beauty. The painter does not rely on the mere brilliance of his colours, but on the particular design of which they form part; nor does the musician concentrate on the mere physical impact of the sounds he is using. The decisive factor governing the meaning of these physical components is their effect upon our emotions. (Once again, we see an analogy between Rousseau's view of art and his attitude towards man's feeling for physical nature, the influence of which is to be measured by its capacity to elicit an emotional response in the beholder.) The successful artist is the one who can organize his physical material in such a way as to produce a certain type of emotional reaction in the spectator; he does not imitate physical objects as such, but the emotions they provoke. Yet this emotional response is inseparable from the effective organization of the physical material, so that the work of art portrays an aspect of the real world transfigured by the power of human feelings.

Although Rousseau admits that the visual arts seem to make a more immediate appeal, since they confront us directly with objects, he considers their impact to be less profound than that of music, because the emotional reaction elicited by a picture will be limited to the visual field. Music, on the other hand, is far less dependent on the idea of physical representation, for although in a general way it may seek to imitate the sounds of nature (storms, songs of birds, etc.), it is much more closely concerned with imitating the emotions associated with certain human situations. Rousseau treats music as a particularly effective way of expressing man's deepest emotions in a pure and simple form. It is for this reason that he goes on to maintain that the essence of music lies in melody rather than harmony. Whereas he deems harmony to be an artificial and intellectual elaboration of pure sensation which produces no more than a complex pattern of physical sound, he believes melody to be much closer to man's natural way of expressing his emotions—his voice; melody, therefore, is most effectively expressed in song. Even when it uses a musical instrument, it must imitate the line and modulations of the human voice in order to produce an emotional response which 'speaks to the heart'. 'All the power of music upon the soul is derived from melody' because the sounds in melody do not simply act upon us as sounds, but as 'signs of our affections, of our feelings'.[1] The contrived complexities of harmony, on the other hand, have no genuine emotional appeal, because they cannot produce anything more than 'mechanical and physical impressions'.

If we examine the nature of melody still more closely, we shall find, says Rousseau in his *Dictionnaire de musique*, that its characteristic way of expressing emotion is through the use of accent, which constitutes, in the words of Dionysius of Halicarnassus, 'the seed of music'.[2] Rousseau's predilection for melody stems from his belief that 'it is from melody alone that there emerges this invincible power of passionate accents' (ii. 132). It is in its use of accent that melody must first 'speak' if it is also to 'sing'. Certainly the musical use of accent is capable of many variations and the superiority of one type of national music over another (for example, the Italian over the French!) will owe a great deal to particular musical skills, but the most important factor of all is the nature of the language used. Rousseau prefers Italian to French as a musical medium, because he believes it to be a language more suitable for song. In any case, he thinks that true music is impossible without the use of words. As both language and music originate in human emotion, the 'accents of melody' and the 'cadence of rhythm' will imitate 'the inflexions which passion gives to the human voice'; in this way, art will 'penetrate the heart and move it by feelings.' Since the power of language and music depends ultimately on the energy of the feelings and the vivacity of the scenes described, they can in favourable circumstances reinforce each other; the great artist will 'make language sing and music speak'.

Although the musical accent expresses the emotion experienced in the presence of objects, these objects may be to a large extent imaginary, so that the musician has greater scope for his creative talent than the visual artist who is limited to the representation of the external world. Being able to draw upon direct emotion, music will have an immediate attraction for 'sensitive hearts and honest souls'.

The need to establish a close link between art and human feeling is at the basis of Rousseau's criticism of the theatre. He does not, of course, deny that the theatre has its own conventions and particular style, but he believes that there ought to be a link between the attitudes and feelings represented on the stage and man's true being. The modern theatre is degenerate because its portrayal of corrupt and pernicious characters gives a false picture of human nature; it ignores the fundamental truth that genuine entertainment must always be closely related to man's true needs and occupations. In spite of its obvious dangers, the theatre, in favourable circumstances, can exercise a beneficial influence on national life. In this connection we recall Rousseau's contrast between the artificial and prison-like character of the contemporary theatre with the form and spirit of Greek tragedy—'these great and superb spectacles, given beneath the sky and in the presence of the whole nation'.[3] Once again, Rousseau stresses the link between entertainment, nature, and the life of the community. Tragedy, for the Greeks, was not something apart from the rest of the nation's life, but an experience through which the people, gathered together in the open air, could 'warm their hearts with feelings of honour and glory'. That is why Greek tragedy always had a harmonious and musical quality that was in keeping with the melodious accent of the Greek language itself. Moreover, when speech, as was the case with the Greeks, contains a musical element, it becomes easier for a good actor to communicate feelings to the 'soul of the sensitive spectator'.

Rousseau's stress upon the simplicity, directness, and unity of true art shows his persistent desire to cut through distinctions and subtleties in order to reach an experience that 'goes directly to the heart'. It also explains his conception of genius. He believes that true genius is capable of rendering genuine emotions in a way that makes them comprehensible to others; the great writer is not concerned primarily with the clever manipulation of words, but with rendering the essence of human feelings.[4] The activity of genius is thus inseparable from that of authentic 'nature'; it is a primordial force which the young artist either has or 'will never know'; true genius can ignore the artifice and corruption of false taste and values in order to reproduce the original power of nature. Although genius needs to be trained and disciplined, it alone has the capacity to do 'great things'.

Some of Rousseau's main ideas about art reappear in his discussion of the problem of language, as is made very clear in his curious *Essai sur l'origine des langues*, upon which we have already drawn for remarks concerning music.[5] Rousseau lays great stress on the idea that the modern use of language for the purpose of social communication or philosophical activity is in many ways a refinement, but also a debasement of its original function. The thinker who wishes to avoid the sterile sophistication and subtlety of the contemporary world must seek to rediscover the authentic roots of language and to relate them to the fundamental aspects of human nature. Rousseau realizes that language, with all its limitations, is an indispensable instrument for the understanding of man's being, provided that it is not treated as an end in itself, but only as part of a deeper human experience.

In many ways Rousseau treats language in the same way as reason: although corrupted by the degeneration of modern life and used for the concealment and distortion of truth rather than for its revelation and communication, language still remains a unique human activity; the philosopher's main problem, therefore, is not to replace it with something else, but to attempt to restore it to its proper function. In this respect, Rousseau's attitude resembles the genetic approach of other thinkers like Locke and Condillac, who relate the emergence of language to the development of the human mind. In *Émile*, for example, he insists that the child's language must be adapted to his psychological condition; consequently, it is pointless to try to teach the language of duty and obligation to a being who can understand nothing but 'force' and 'necessity'. In the *Discours sur l'inégalité* Rousseau deals with the much-discussed question of the historical origins of language, only to conclude that the problem is insoluble. Nevertheless, as the *Essai sur l'origine des langues* makes clear, the key to an adequate conception of language is to be found only in a consideration of its original purpose. Although language has undoubtedly suffered from the general perversion of human values, and linguistic refinement has been used for unworthy ends such as sterile ratiocination or the jargon of a society dominated by artificial and corrupt passions, the restoration of the true function of language requires a careful investigation of its relationship with its original elements and their bearing upon the expression of man's primordial needs.

A study of the origins of language, in so far as it is feasible, suggests that 'man's first cry is the cry of nature', and that the primary function of language is to express feelings and emotions rather than thoughts and ideas. Consequently, primitive languages did not have the limited intellectual range of modern ones, but were used to express man's primary needs. Although language was originally expressive, it also had a communicative aspect, for a cry might serve to call attention to the presence of an object involved in the satisfaction of some elemental impulse; the cry itself could be accompanied by the use of gesture and signs. Indeed, a sign would be more immediately effective than a sound. 'The most energetic language is the one in which the sign has said everything before we speak' (*Essai*, p. 31). Visual signs have the great advantage of making a direct appeal to the imagination; as Rousseau points out in *Émile*, 'by neglecting the language of the signs which speak to the imagination, people have lost the most energetic of languages' (iv. 645). The excessive use of reason and verbal precepts has weakened the original power of sign-language. When people of old used signs rather than language, they did not speak but showed what they meant. How much more effective was the gesture of Diogenes walking before Zeno or of Tarquin cutting off the heads of the poppies than the longest and most eloquent discourse! The chief limitation of signs is that they do not allow for the expression of deep emotional needs; it is sounds, rather than gestures, which 'move the heart and inflame the passions'. (*Essai*, p. 35) As men grew closer together and came to know more complex emotional needs, they needed to develop a language capable of expressing them. Yet the oldest languages depended upon their natural content—euphony, harmony, and beauty of sound as well as 'voices, sounds, accents, and number', so that the use of one element did not mean the exclusion of the rest. The language of accent is particularly important, for 'the accent is the soul of discourse and gives it feeling and truth' (iv. 296). (In this respect, Rousseau's view of language coincides with his attitude towards music.) The invention of writing as a means of stabilizing language seriously impaired its original function by making it subservient to reflection and abstraction instead of allowing it to express the human feelings for which it was first intended. Reflection destroyed the poetic force of language. More important still, it led to a serious differentiation of activities which had until then been united. Primitive peoples, for example, did not consider poetry to be a specialized activity, but treated poetry, music, and discourse as aspects of the same fundamental experience. 'Verse, song, and words have a common origin.' Rousseau refers with approval to Strabo's statement that in the ancient world 'speaking and singing were the same thing' (*Essai*, p. 141). How different from the language of today! The 'progress of reasoning' and the 'perfecting of grammar' have unfortunately destroyed the 'singing' quality of the older languages. Indeed, the very separation of eloquence, poetry, and music into distinct arts is a sure indication of their decline.

Rousseau tirelessly insists upon the great energy of ancient languages. The enfeeblement of modern man is mirrored in the debasement of his language; the vigour of soul, which was evident in the character of the ancients and is so markedly absent from modern life,[6] was a dominant feature of ancient languages. The modern preacher or academician has difficulty in making himself heard in a confined space, while the generals of old harangued whole armies without difficulty; Herodotus 'used to read his history to the peoples of Greece assembled in the open air' (*Essai*, p. 199). It was not a question of physical strength but of a different moral attitude; the orators of old effortlessly attuned themselves to their physical environment and to the minds and souls of their hearers, because they were all animated by the same human feelings. 'Any language with which one cannot make oneself understood to the assembled nations is a servile language' (*Essai*. p. 201). Our language is the language of slaves; the language of the ancients was the language of free men.

Rousseau, then, is reluctant to consider art as an isolated, specialized activity carried out by a few performers and watched by passive spectators. Since it must derive from 'man's nature, his work and his pleasures', it must also involve his relations with other people. Attention has already been called to the way in which Rousseau, in the *Lettre à d'Alembert*, dreams of the day when his fellow Genevans will be able to participate in national celebrations inspired by feelings which are both patriotic and human. Unlike the dark cavern of the modern theatre with its timid, motionless audience lost in silence and inaction, happy people rejoice in the spontaneous expression of their emotions and the beauty of physical nature. Of the Genevan entertainments, he says: 'Let them be free and generous as you, let the sun cast its light upon your innocent pleasures'.[7] The similarity between the setting and spirit of the ancient Greek tragedy and those of the ideal Genevan *fêtes* is unmistakable. In each case we are transported to a land of 'peace, freedom, equity, and innocence' where every citizen shares fully in the 'simplicity' and 'secret charm' of national life.

A still more striking, though equally idealized, example of Rousseau's effort to regenerate art and language by bringing them closer to nature is to be found in the description of the grape-harvest in *La Nouvelle Héloïse*.[8] Here again we are in the presence of a collective activity—'people gather together in order to go to the vineyard'—and the whole community of Clarens takes part in an experience that combines work and play, the useful and the pleasant. Amid 'the simplicity of pastoral and country life' and 'all the charms of the golden age', everything contributes to 'the pleasant moving spectacle of the general gladness which seems to extend over the face of the earth'. The spirit of joyful abundance inspires the happy workers to singing, story-telling, and (later in the day) dancing. Their songs are based on 'simple, naïve, often sad and yet pleasing words'. On all sides can be heard the 'concert' of voices singing in unison. (Even in a letter such as this, Rousseau cannot help castigating the contemporary love of harmony as a sure sign of 'depraved taste', and pointing out that nothing is more contrary to the 'impulse of nature'!) At Clarens song, speech, and laughter mingle with other sounds such as the hooping of casks and vats, the continual tramping of the harvesters bringing the grapes to the wine-press, and the 'hoarse sound of the rustic instruments inciting them to work'. All these different sounds seem to be but part of a single scene in which freedom and equality combine to form a joyous festive air. 'The secret equality' of this busy community suggests that man has at last discovered his real nature and with it a language capable of giving outward expression to all the feelings of his innermost soul.

Notes

1. Cf. *Essai sur l'origine des langues où il est parlé de la mélodie et de l'imitation musicale*, ed. C. Porset (Bordeaux, 1968), p. 163. (Quoted hereafter as *Essai*.)

2. Article, 'Accent'.

3. *Lettre à a'Alembert*. p. 105. Cf. above, p. 24.

4. Cf. articles, 'Goût' and 'Génie', in the *Dictionnaire de musique*.

5. See above, p. 128 n. 1; the full title is significant.

6. Cf. above, p. 21.

7. *Lettre à d'Alembert* (ed. Fuchs), p. 168.

8. There is a detailed commentary on this episode by Bernard Guyon in *Oeuvres*, ii. 602–11. 1707–14, as well as by Jean Starobinski in a valuable section of his *Jean-Jacques Rousseau: la transparence et l'obstacle*, pp. 114 ff.

9
The Problem of Personal Existence

THE relation between Rousseau's personal writings and didactic treatises is obviously not a simple one, since works which were inspired by complex psychological motives cannot have the same philosophical significance as those which were intended for the enlightenment of humanity. Nevertheless, the personal writings cannot be ignored in any general consideration of Rousseau's ideas, for these, as we have seen, were not meant to be merely abstract speculations but contributions to the fuller understanding of human experience. From the outset Rousseau had drawn inspiration from his own heart and found philosophical truth in the depth of his own being. Since his view of man cannot be completely separated from his existence as an individual thinker, it would obviously be imprudent to ignore the general significance of works which, though primarily concerned with the analysis of his own personality, had repercussions upon his attitude towards human nature. Moreover, a consideration of the personal writings, as recent 'thematic' studies of Rousseau have shown, may help to bring out certain basic preoccupations which are apt to elude a merely intellectual approach to his work; his personal writings express deep feelings which, though occupying only a subordinate place in the didactic writings because they lie below the surface of systematic reflection, may have helped to shape his philosophical ideas. In order to obtain an adequate conception of his thought, it is necessary to examine all the factors—personal and philosophical—which helped to determine his general attitude towards existence.

In the preamble to the *Confessions* Rousseau seeks to bring out the human significance of his self-analysis: he affirms that no previous writer has had the courage or honesty to explore the individual 'in all the truth of nature'; he claims to be producing the 'sole human portrait exactly according to nature, which exists or probably ever will exist' (i. 3). Yet he considers that such a work will also be useful, because it will serve as the 'primary criterion' for the study of man; this unique portrait can thus become an example of universal truth. Nevertheless, Rousseau's attempt to give the *Confessions* general human significance soon yields to the influence of personal motives of more restricted import. Even the role of the readers to whom the work is directed tends to become subordinated to Rousseau's interest in his own personal problem. The 'I alone' which stands at the head of the second paragraph of the *Confessions*, as well as the subsequent statement: 'I am made like none of the men I have seen ... I dare to believe that I am made like none of those that exist' (i. 5), offer a salutary warning to anyone seeking to draw some general conclusion from this unique undertaking. Moreover, the real significance of Rousseau's attitude towards other people is brought out in his observation at the very end of the same paragraph, where he exhorts the 'fellow men' for whom the portrait of Jean-Jacques is intended, to imagine themselves at the feet of God's throne, asking whether they are 'better than that man'. Clearly Rousseau's main concern is not with making his reader aware of his own humanity as such, but with inducing him to make a comparison between himself and the writer of the *Confessions*: in this way the reader will come to realize that his ultimate responsibility is to pass judgement on Jean-Jacques's character; the presence of the words 'that man' at the very end of the sentence indicates the person upon whom the reader must finally focus his attention. It follows that the other person does not exist solely as Jean-Jacques's impartial judge, but as one who, after comparing himself with the defendant, will undoubtedly exonerate the latter from all wickedness.[1]

The *Confessions* not only seek to fix an image of Jean-Jacques which will be accepted by the reader-judge as an authentic likeness; they are also intended to destroy the false image which Rousseau believes to exist in other people's minds. Already in the letters written to M. de Malesherbes in 1762 he had revealed his overwhelming need to do this, while his very last work, the *Rêveries*, betrays the same obsessive desire to eliminate the 'imaginary and fantastic being' created by people who 'judged his feelings and heart by theirs' (i. 1130, 1152); wrongly considering him to be a misanthropist, they had simply failed to realise his true character as a lover of freedom and a man devoted to the enjoyment of his own being. Yet this false image could not be effectively destroyed until it had been replaced by the portrait of the good Jean-Jacques.

Self-analysis and self-justification are bound up with an equally strong desire for self-expression. By writing his *Confessions* Rousseau not only wanted to know himself and alleviate his guilt, he sought also to recapture the happiness of the past, to savour again those brief but precious occasions when he felt that he had been truly himself and had lived as nature had wanted. He readily acknowledged his pleasure in dwelling on those rare moments of complete personal fulfilment.

Yet any man's attempt to present an authentic image of himself raises certain difficulties, as Rousseau admits in the first draft of the *Confessions*. Although the individual, who knows himself better than anyone else, is in a privileged position for describing his own being, he is also the one most liable to disguise it: 'he shows himself as he wants to be seen' (i. 1149). Rousseau thinks that he has solved this difficulty in his own case, not only by his greater honesty, but also by the very form of his work. He admits that a mere account of the events of his life would often be defective and, more important still, that the meaning of actions and circumstances would be confined to the deceptive world of appearances. Since the error of his contemporaries was to mistake appearance for reality, their corrupt and inadequate standards would certainly make them incapable of understanding the real Jean-Jacques. Rousseau believes that his true personality is not expressed by his actions, but only by something that can be known and experienced more directly—his feelings. As he says, he may make mistakes about the events of his life, but never about the feelings accompanying them; these feelings are still alive, for they form part of his inner being. In writing his confessions, therefore, he is not recounting the history of the events themselves but the 'secret history of his soul'. (Moreover, he is convinced that his social situation as a man of the people who has known all classes of men, of both low and high degree, has let him penetrate beneath the mask and see the real human being concealed underneath.) If he stresses the idea of a secret history, it is not only because events may often be at variance with feelings, but also because feelings may be of various kinds and originate in some deeper initial impulse which has been subsequently forgotten. Rousseau stresses 'the thread of secret dispositions', the 'train of secret affections', which hold together the various psychological components of his personality (i. 1149–50).

Apart from being hidden, the inner cause of events may be obscure or inconsistent with the rest of a man's character, so that it is not easy to obtain knowledge of the 'inner model' responsible for his actions. Did not Jean-Jacques himself behave on many occasions in a bizarre and irrational way which made him unlike himself? At such times he 'became another man and ceased to be himself' (i. 417). Such a metamorphosis could be for good or evil: he might be blinded by a sudden illumination, as happened on the road to Vincennes when he was suddenly vouchsafed a vision of 'all the contradictions of the social system' and saw 'another universe' (a favourite expression) and became another man. At other times, his behaviour could be equally degrading: such was the case with his false accusation against the servant-girl Marion. He acknowledged that his personality was given to abrupt changes of mood, to extraordinary psychological 'oscillations' (his own word), which he had already noted in the light-hearted self-portrait contributed to the first and only number of *Le Persifleur*, the journal he and Diderot once intended to produce together: he had there spoken of his 'weekly souls'. 'Nothing is so unlike me as myself ... A Proteus, a cameleon, a woman are beings less changeable than I' (i. 1108). At the same time he did not doubt the persistence of 'certain dominant dispositions and certain almost periodic returns' which conferred an essential coherence upon his personality.

The psychological purpose of the *Confessions* can be best served, thinks Rousseau, by following the chronological method and by describing events and feelings as they occurred. The honest detailed description of these moods, however complex or contradictory they may be, will eventually allow the real man to emerge. Rousseau believes that such a method has the advantage of letting the reader 'perceive the first features imprinted in his [Rousseau's] soul', for his character is such that, since memories and feelings take precedence over events and objects, the initial impression determines all the rest. As he says at the end of the fourth book of the *Confessions*, 'there is a certain succession of affections and ideas which modify the ones that follow and which must be known in order to be properly judged'. If he gives a full account of the 'first causes', their connection with subsequent effects will be made plain. In this way he hopes 'in some way to make his soul transparent to the reader's eyes'; that is why he has tried to depict himself from all points of view and to reveal his character in every light (i. 174–5). Already in the second book he had affirmed his intention of 'keeping himself constantly before his reader's eyes'. 'Nothing in me must remain obscure or hidden'; the reader must follow him 'in all the aberrations of his heart, in all the recesses of his life; he must not lose sight of him for a single moment' (i. 59).

Yet the purpose of this complete self-revelation is made clear by a further point: the chronological account will not be accompanied by any direct attempt to determine the meaning of his character; he will not say: 'This is the man I am.' It is the reader who must have the responsibility of deciding the meaning of Rousseau's character; 'it is his task to gather together the elements and to determine the being constituted by them' (i. 175). Rousseau will thus have the satisfaction of knowing that he has been frank and honest and yet freed from the burden of passing judgement upon his own character; it is the other man who will have to be the judge, because it is he who will have created the portrait of the real Rousseau. The latter will be able to rest secure in the knowledge that he has fully revealed himself, and yet be reassured by the thought that the authenticity of the portrait thus produced is guaranteed by the reader himself.

Nevertheless, the *Confessions* could achieve their purpose only if

Rousseau found people capable of responding to his self-portrait in the way he desired. This he unfortunately failed to do. When he followed a public reading of the work with a statement challenging anyone to say that he was a 'dishonest man', he encountered nothing but a disconcerting silence. The official ban placed by the authorities on any further reading of the work served only to increase his anxiety and confusion. Thrust back into himself, he was confronted by the desperate need to justify himself once more. The result was the composition of the *Dialogues: Rousseau juge de Jean-Jacques*. These dialogues are between 'Rousseau', a would-be seeker of the truth about Jean-Jacques (in fact, an obvious sympathizer) and the 'Frenchman', a basically honest but gullible victim of Jean-Jacques's slanderers; the true characters of the work, however, are the ones who do not appear directly, but are described in the course of the dialogues —the innocent and misunderstood 'Jean-Jacques' and his implacable enemies, 'the gentlemen' responsible for the plot against him. Apart from the obvious change in literary form, the *Dialogues* differ from the *Confessions* in their presentation of Rousseau's character: the gradual destruction of the false Jean-Jacques is eventually followed by a fully rounded portrait of the real man—a portrait which we, like Rousseau and the Frenchman, are asked to accept as genuine. In one way, however, this direct portrait, when it is compared with the character described in the *Confessions*, represents a curiously simplified Rousseau who is henceforth identified with 'the man of nature'. His enemies' greatest mistake, he affirms, is to have made him into a complex, calculating being, whereas he is, in fact, *l'homme sensible* concerned mainly with the 'enjoyment of himself and his existence'; 'occupied with and by himself', he lives 'completely for himself' and 'wishes to enjoy and seek his entire happiness within'. Accordingly, he follows the impulse of nature rather than the call for virtue, for virtue has no great meaning for a man who obeys his sensibility and leads in solitude 'an even, simple, and routine life' remarkable for its uniformity and gentleness. He does not look to the future, but lives from day to day, happy to accept the yoke of nature rather than the will of man; living in the immediate present, he 'gives himself completely to each feeling which moves him'; his greatest bliss is to be 'at his ease', to let himself be carried along by the spontaneous impulse of his senses and feelings and to remain effortlessly responsive to the sights and sounds of nature. (Cf. i. 861–5 and *passim*.)

Yet this new 'man of nature' is very different from the primitive creature living in the state of nature. Not only is his sensibility more highly developed but he also experiences a much greater need to indulge in expansive feelings. Whereas primitive man was content to follow the impulse of self-preservation and natural pity, Rousseau admits that his solitude is to some extent imposed upon him by adversity. Essentially he is an affectionate man obsessed by 'this need to love which devoured his heart from childhood'. If he now longs for life in the next world, it is because he hopes to find there 'a fatherland and friends in a better order of things' (i. 827). Even the enjoyment of his feelings for nature is to some extent (as he admits) a mere substitute for the human affection of which he feels himself to be so unhappily deprived. Cut off from his fellow men, he tries to satisfy his longing for love by living in the domain of his imagination where he can enjoy the intimacy of a 'society of beings after his own heart'. A still greater difference between Rousseau and primitive man is to be found in the way in which his imaginative activity is associated with the dream of perfection; in his lonely reveries he seeks 'harmony, beauty, and perfection', just as in his didactic work he had wanted to make men aware of 'perfections of all kinds'. 'His cherished images will be permeated by the immortal charms of perfection.' The simple spontaneity of Jean-Jacques's character is thus deemed to be compatible with the activity of a highly developed sensibility which derives satisfaction from the enjoyment of its own idealistic aspirations.

Rousseau finds support for this notion of himself as a sensitive and imaginative man of uninhibited natural impulse in the world described at the very beginning of the *Dialogues*, 'an ideal world like ours and yet very different' (i. 668). There nature is the same as on this earth, but it has a vividness, clarity, purity, and simplicity that are lacking in everyday life. Because the first movements of nature are good and right and impel us towards our preservation and happiness, the inhabitants of this world will be content to follow the 'gentle and primitive passions which spring from *amour de soi*'. Their virtue is different from that of social beings, since it does not involve any conflict with nature. Such people will certainly have faults and vices, but they will come from weakness and indolence and an inability to triumph over obstacles rather than from deliberate wickedness. Their goal is not the superficial 'appearance' of society, but 'intimate feelings' and the 'art of personal enjoyment'; they wish to *be* rather than to *have*, to seek the pleasure of enjoyment rather than the anxiety of possession (i. 672). It is not surprising to find the Frenchman naïvely telling 'Monsieur Rousseau' that he resembles the inhabitants of this world, while Monsieur Rousseau, in his turn, modestly admits that, whether this be so or not, the author of *Émile* and *La Nouvelle Héloïse* ought certainly to be counted among them! At the same time, Rousseau adds a further significant detail to the personal image when he tries to give it some objective significance by extending it to a select company of like-minded people, an élite of 'initiates' who will recognize their brethren without the intermediary of language, for they will be immediately aware of the meaning of certain signs and gestures known only to themselves. In all this Rousseau places increasing stress upon the idea of a complete, direct experience of personal being.

Having discovered his authentic self and related it to a more general conception of nature, Rousseau believes that he will henceforth be able to lead a contemplative life that banishes all tormenting reflection and lets him 'enjoy at his ease all the felicity of which he feels the power and need within himself'; he will be able to avoid the painful inner conflicts which tear apart those who 'eagerly tread the social path' and allow themselves to be distracted by the 'tumult of societies' (i. 823). Following his heart rather than his conscience, he will not need to expose himself to 'the toil and struggle of virtue'. However, the greatest attraction of this view of himself as a man of nature is in the profound sense of inner unity and peace it engenders; he is now at one with himself, completely identified with what he immediately is.

Yet this search for personal authenticity is based on an overwhelming need not only for unity but also for the triumph of his goodness and innocence. Rousseau is henceforth a man who, being good and innocent, cannot be accused of wickedness. If he is a man of sensibility rather than reflection, it is because reflection is associated with the evils of society—evils from which Rousseau has been miraculously preserved by his simple nature. The truth is, however, that he has been able to achieve this personal unity and innocence only by polarizing the notion of good and evil in an absolute way: goodness is identified with Jean-Jacques, while evil, being associated with the existence of his implacable enemies and the universal plot of which they are originators, is attributed to something outside himself. Guilt and evil have been expelled from Rousseau's conscious mind by a psychological mechanism which makes them seem quite external to his own being.

Yet this image of the innocent and self-sufficient man of nature surrounded by ruthless enemies is often presented in an intense, frenzied mood. In no other work has Rousseau been the victim of such nightmarish psychological tension. The style and tone of the *Dialogues* show that their author is not the calm, simple man of nature portrayed in them, but a tormented being desperately anxious to fight off inner contradictions and conflicts. It is only towards the end of the work that Rousseau can claim to have found some degree of inner peace by adopting an attitude of resignation towards his desperate situation.

That the composition of the *Dialogues* did not bring him peace is proved by the extraordinary events which followed their completion and which Rousseau himself has chronicled in the 'History of the preceding work' appended to the main text. At first he searched desperately for a suitable person to whom he could entrust his manuscript. After first placing his hopes in the philosopher Condillac and the young Englishman Brooke Boothby, he finally decided to put his trust in God by depositing the work on the high altar of the Cathedral of Notre Dame. The frustration of this attempt reduced him to a state of acute panic which he tried to overcome by distributing to passers-by a pamphlet entitled: 'To any Frenchman still loving justice and truth'. He eventually achieved some degree of inner resignation when he asked himself the vital question: 'Is the essence of my being in their looks?' (i. 985). For a moment he was able to shake off the hostile influence of other people's gaze and believe that the testimony of his conscience would be strong enough to protect him against the machinations of his enemies and make him indifferent to any harm they might still seek to inflict upon him; he was finally convinced that the image of Jean-Jacques which existed in other people's minds was no longer a matter of concern to him, since he would now remain content with his own immediate being.

Yet the restless activity of self-consciousness could not be so easily stilled. The *Dialogues* were followed by a renewal of literary activity which produced the unfinished *Rêveries du promeneur solitaire*. It is significant that the very first paragraph of the new work contains the question: 'What am I?'—which is all the more remarkable when we recall the hundreds of pages Rousseau had already devoted to answering it. The composition of the *Confessions* and *Dialogues* had plainly failed to appease the persistent and anxious need for reflection and self-examination. However, the form of the *Rêveries* reveals an important change of emphasis: Rousseau now abandons any attempt to present a systematic and complete portrait of himself; he will henceforth compose 'a shapeless diary'. The Promenades which constitute the *Rêveries* are in the form of essays prompted by some personal reflection which has occurred to him during his lonely walks. No doubt the antithesis between the good Jean-Jacques and his wicked enemies still forms the psychological basis of his observations, for it is too firmly implanted in his mind ever to be eradicated; as is clear from the second sentence of the work, with its reference to 'the most sociable and loving of human beings' who has been 'proscribed by an unanimous agreement', the personal writings will seek to keep intact to the very end the image of the good and innocent Rousseau. In spite of his occasional obsession with the thought of his enemies and the 'hellish' and 'devilish' ruses by which they seek to 'bury him alive', the theme of persecution is not now so obsessive as to prevent him from dwelling on the more positive side of his character and undertaking a further exploration of his inner life. The diary may be shapeless, but he claims that it will not lack precision, for it will consist of detailed personal observations which will be as accurate as the scientist's recording of changes in barometric pressure; he will seek to keep a 'faithful register' of the 'modifications of his soul and their consequences' without trying to reduce them to a system (i. 1000).

Although this self-analysis is still meant to provide yet another 'monument of his innocence', it is not intended primarily for other people, especially his persecutors, whom he now professes to treat as inanimate objects, or, in his own curious expression, as 'differently moved masses' of matter. More important still is his avowed intention of ignoring the fate of his manuscript; he will no longer worry about its possible theft or mutilation. 'Delivered from the anxiety of hope', he is now writing solely for himself. 'Alone for the rest of my life, I find consolation, hope, and peace only in myself; I must and wish to be no longer occupied except with myself'; henceforth he will 'feed on his own substance' (i. 999). Writing is now indissolubly linked with personal experience and the satisfaction of 'conversing with his own soul'; any wider implications it may have are purely incidental. He admits that he may hope to obtain some moral benefit from his self-analysis. His exclusion of the notion of virtue is not as rigorous as in the other personal writings; he is going to undertake a 'unique and useful study', so that he may one day leave this life not 'better', but more 'virtuous', than when he entered it (i. 1023); it is 'never too late to prepare oneself for the account that one will eventually have to give of oneself', and Rousseau hopes to 'redress his errors and reform his will'; he will learn to be 'wise, truthful, modest, and less presumptuous'. At one point he concedes that he may have been guilty of self-deception and that he is less virtuous than he had once supposed; he agrees that for a man who adopts the motto *Vitam impendere vero* ('to sacrifice one's life to truth'),[2] lying is inexcusable, even on the grounds of weakness. Henceforth he will seek to avoid such moral lapses.

These moral considerations, however, are much less important than a much more steadfast purpose—that of finding a form of personal happiness which will sustain him for the rest of his life. In this connection, it may be helpful to consider briefly this particular conception of happiness in the light of his general view of the matter. Although less systematic than his other personal writings, the *Rêveries* place the same emphasis upon happiness as an immediate and enduring personal experience; they are still concerned with achieving a mode of existence suited to the 'man of nature' described in the *Dialogues*. Rousseau always believed that happiness was inseparable from the reality of immediate experience; in its complete form it went beyond reflection and language. Describing his happiness with Mme de Warens Rousseau stated in the *Confessions*: 'But how can I describe what was neither said nor done, nor even thought, but felt, without my evoking any other object of my happiness than this feeling itself? ... Happiness followed me everywhere; it was not in any specific thing: it was complete in myself, it could not leave me for a single moment' (i. 225). Already in the second *Discours* he had described primitive man as a being who was able to abandon himself completely to 'the immediate feeling of his present existence'. Nevertheless, at this rudimentary level, the spontaneous nature of the experience tends to give it the form of a passive abandonment to some instinctive impulse; even when there is a more positive assertion of the self (as in the case of certain forms of self-preservation), it still remains a blind impulse devoid of genuine reflection. Primitive man, therefore, does not *know* that he is happy; he *is* happy. Although his potential capacity for freedom and perfectibility already distinguishes him sharply from the animals, his life is still based on the satisfaction of immediate needs.

The fully developed individual, on the other hand, requires a much higher form of happiness. Although he still seeks to remain faithful to his own nature and to identify himself with his immediate being, he also feels a powerful need to establish relations with other people and the external world; to some extent he must always move outside himself; he is impelled towards others by his inability to live solely on his own inner resources. From this weakness comes, as Rousseau insists, his happiness. In the didactic works, this expansive aspect of the human personality is related, as we have seen, to a conception of existence based on the principle of order; the wise and virtuous man's being reflects the moral principle discernible in the general scheme of things, so that the virtue achieved through the activity of the will helps the individual to take his place in the universal order. In practical terms, however, this involves some restriction on emotion and sensibility, for the individual may be required to sacrifice immediate satisfaction for the sake of the general good.

Yet Rousseau could never completely overcome his feeling that virtue was, to some extent, a regrettable necessity rather than a positive source of happiness—an unfortunate consequence of man's need to accept the limitations of social life. When, in his own personal life, he felt himself cut off from the rest of the community, he very readily accepted the idea that true happiness consisted of the self's immediate enjoyment of its uninhibited feelings. This personal experience could not be satisfied with the mere contemplation of physical nature or the limitations imposed upon it by such an attitude: Rousseau felt a powerful need to identify himself with the universal system in a positive, intense way. We have already had occasion to observe how his feeling for nature impelled him towards the spiritual origin of the physical world; the beauty of the creation filled him with an ecstatic sense of wonder and admiration and at the same time made him want to move closer to it.

Yet this expansive movement towards the spiritual essence of God's universe awakened strong religious feelings which took the form of a desire for the infinite. When judged by human standards, this longing for perfection seemed capable of only negative expression and was apt to produce a sense of inner void in the presence of what was beyond man's experience. This yearning for the infinite is very apparent in the famous third letter to Malesherbes. Rousseau there describes an apparently ideal day in his existence—a day when, freed from worldly cares, he enjoyed a blissful solitude in the midst of nature. His greatest delight, he declares, was to be alone with 'the whole of nature and its inconceivable author' (i. 1130). Yet, in spite of the happiness obtained from exploring nature in all her beauty, his imagination could not remain satisfied with her as she was: he felt an overwhelming need to 'populate her with beings after his own heart'. Nature was transformed into the abode of a 'charming society of which he did not feel himself to be unworthy'. 'I formed a golden age according to my fancy.' Memories of the happy past and dreams of perfect bliss formed the basis of this paradisaic existence by filling out the empty spaces of the real world. Nevertheless, Rousseau himself was aware of the inadequacy of his escapist feelings.

'In the midst of all that, I admit, the nothingness of my dreams would sometimes come and suddenly make my soul sad.' He goes on: 'Even though all my dreams had been turned into realities, they would not have been enough for me: I should have imagined, dreamed, desired still more. Within myself I found an inexplicable void which nothing could have filled—a certain yearning of the heart for another kind of enjoyment of which I had no idea and yet of which I felt the need' (i. 1140). He is careful to add that this craving for the unattainable was not a painful experience, since it contained 'a very lively feeling and an alluring sadness which I should not have wanted to be without'. At the same time he felt himself being transported beyond the domain of language and reflection to the contemplation of 'all the beings of nature, the universal system of things and the incomprehensible Being who encompasses everything'. Just as he had refused to rest content with the dreams of his own inner world, so was he now unable to limit himself to the physical world, however entrancing its form. 'I was stifling in the universe, I should have liked to soar up into the infinite.' The mood culminated in an attitude of speechless adoration before the majesty of God and His creation. In 'the excitement of his transports' he could do nothing but exclaim: 'O great Being! O great Being!'

Since unsatisfied longing thus gave way to ecstatic delight, Jean-Jacques considered that days such as these formed 'his life's true happiness—happiness without bitterness, without tedium, without regrets, to which I should willingly have confined the happiness of my whole existence' (i. 1142). Indeed, at such times, he seemed to obtain a glimpse of the meaning of eternity, for he did not believe that even the 'celestial intelligences' could experience more 'ravishing contemplations'.

At a more restricted psychological level, Rousseau had already stressed in *Émile* the negative and subjective implications of man's experience of perfection, whether of love or beauty. The activity of his imagination takes him beyond finite reality towards an elusive but enchanting world of perfect fulfilment. Yet this world remains shadowy and unsubstantial, because the object of man's aspirations is beautified by his own dreams and longings. Thus 'there is nothing beautiful save what is not' (iv. 821; ii. 693). Sometimes the enthusiasm of perfect love may be animated by a merely chimerical object 'existing in the imagination'. 'All is illusion in love and its only reality consists of the feeling inspiring it' (iv. 743).

Man's moments of complete happiness are constantly threatened by the renewal of his desire for infinite perfection and the longing for an unattainable ideal. Julie, in *La Nouvelle Héloïse*, makes this very clear. For a time her existence seems to have attained complete fulfilment; she experiences all the elements of Rousseau's own ideal conception of happiness: plenitude, absolute inner unity, shared intimacy, harmonious and expansive relationship with the immediate environment, and the spontaneous realization of all possible desires in an experience that is vivid and immediate:

I am surrounded by everything that concerns me, the whole universe is here for me; I enjoy both the attachment I have for my friends and their attachment to me and one another.... I see nothing which does not extend my being and nothing which divides it; it is in everything around me; there remains no part of it which is far from me. My imagination has nothing more to do, I have nothing more to desire: to feel and to enjoy are for me the same thing: at the same time I live in all that I love, and I am absolutely full of life's happiness. (ii. 689)

Yet she is subsequently forced to admit that this experience cannot give her complete satisfaction, and the account of perfect bliss is followed by an astonishing invocation of death. 'O death, come when you will! I fear you no longer!' Even more surprising is her observation at the very moment when her happiness seems to be complete: 'Happiness bores me!' Within herself she feels 'an inexplicable void' and a remarkable 'emptiness of soul'. The satisfaction of desire seems to have brought only the destruction of happiness. It is as though the attainment of a particular goal is immediately followed by a feeling of dissatisfaction and the need to replace it by the pursuit of another. As Julie points out, it is the constant but vain effort to satisfy this lack which constitutes the ultimate meaning of existence:

Woe to him who has nothing more to desire! he loses, so to speak, all he possesses. One enjoys less what one obtains than what one hopes for, and one is happy only before being happy. Illusion ceases at the point where enjoyment begins. The land of fancy is in this world the only one worthy of being inhabited, and such is the nothingness of human things that apart from the Being who exists by himself, there is nothing beautiful save what is not. (ii. 693)

The problem is given a religious solution in *La Nouvelle Héloïse*, because Julie dies and finds absolute bliss in the next life. The occasional experience of an 'inexplicable void' thus does not create a permanent problem for Rousseau, for such moments are absorbed into a more fundamental religious mood. In the end, the desire for immediate fulfilment and complete personal unity is stronger than the movement towards infinite perfection. It is also noteworthy that the power of spontaneous feeling and the reality of personal experience, even when they assume a specifically religious form, retain their essentially human characteristics, inasmuch as they still express the desire for perfect inner unity and plenitude. In a sense Julie welcomes death as a mere prelude to complete and unalloyed bliss in the next world; the Vicaire too, as we have seen, relates his hope of immortality to his dreams of personal fulfilment. Whatever the particular expression of his desire for happiness, Rousseau always stresses the idea of absolute and immediate plenitude.

This yearning for immediate happiness is not surprising in view of the psychological tensions which prompted Rousseau to compose the personal writings, for he was constantly seeking inner peace and unity rather than the indefinite extension of his dreams. Not only is this already apparent in the portrait of the man of nature given in the *Dialogues*, but the same theme re-emerges very clearly in his last work, where he speaks of his desires to be 'fully himself, himself without diversion, without obstacle ... to be what nature wanted' (i. 1002). Truly personal existence is the experience of plenitude, the condition of a being that is full of nothing but itself.

It is in the famous fifth Promenade that Rousseau gives his most elaborate account of the pure 'feeling of existence'. As an absolute experience, it goes beyond the normal consciousness of time and space. After describing man's position as a victim of time and as a being tormented by regret for the past or anxiety for the future—as a being 'behind' or 'ahead' of himself—Rousseau gives an account of perfect reverie:

But if there is a state in which the soul finds a basis that is solid enough for it to rest entirely in it and gather there its entire being, without any need to recall the past or anticipate the future; in which time is nothing for it, in which the present always endures without marking its duration and without any trace of succession, without any other feeling of privation or enjoyment, of pleasure or pain, desire or fear than that of our existence alone; and if this feeling alone can fill the soul entirely, then, as long as this state lasts, the one who experiences it can call himself happy, not with an imperfect, poor, and relative happiness but with a sufficient, perfect and full happiness which leaves in the soul no void which it feels the need to fill. (i. 1046)

He goes on to say that in such a situation one enjoys

nothing external to oneself, nothing except oneself and one's own existence; as long as this state lasts, one is self-sufficient like God. The feeling of existence deprived of any other affection is of itself a precious feeling of contentment and peace which would alone be enough to make this existence dear and sweet to the man who knew how to remove all the sensual earthly impressions which constantly come and distract us from it and disturb its sweetness here below. (i. 1047)

The main characteristics of this mood are, first of all, its completeness and self-sufficiency. In reverie man finds absolute fulfilment and security, with no need to move beyond immediate experience. Normal temporal divisions are overcome, for there is no thought of the past or future; the self is identified with a kind of eternal present which excludes any anxious concern with the passing of time. Instead of time, it is more appropriate to speak of 'duration', for it is a kind of complete experience without any of the ephemeral characteristics of everyday time. Moreover, it lacks the psychological limitations of normal temporal experience, which takes the form of hope, anxiety, or regret, and for most men involves the need to overcome some kind of inner lack or sense of insufficiency. The state of reverie knows no such limitations, because it does not look beyond itself but is 'sufficient, perfect, and full'. It differs from ordinary experience in that it does not involve the enjoyment of anything outside the self; the feeling of immediate personal existence provides its own unique happiness. This is why it seems to possess the privileged self-sufficiency of the divine being, the only being existing by himself.

It does not seem, however, as though this experience is, in any proper religious sense, mystical. When he says that 'one is self-sufficient like God', Rousseau is simply using a very forceful analogy. The self suddenly obtains a fleeting glimpse of the essential quality of the divine being; it does not identify itself with God, for it is absorbed in itself. Even the 'natural mysticism' sometimes attributed to Rousseau is not a genuine aspect of this experience. It is only the sensuous aspect of the self which pulsates gently to the rhythm of nature; as Rousseau sits on the shore of the Lake of Bienne, his senses are 'fixed' by the 'uniform and moderate movement' of the water; this gentle involvement of the senses is a mere prelude to the liberation of his higher self for the enjoyment of its own existence. The same process occurs in connection with feeling and reflection: heart and mind are not allowed to fall into complete torpor, for this would simply destroy the activity of consciousness. The emotions are subjected to no disturbing 'agitation'; they simply respond to the 'ebb and flow' of the water. In the same way without taking the trouble to think, the mind lets occasional thoughts flit across its surface: brief reflections about the instability of the world are appropriately suggested by the rippling water. Yet these reactions are not important in themselves but mainly as a means of creating conditions which will eventually allow self-consciousness to operate in complete peace and security.

The perfection of this experience probably owes something to the creative activity of Rousseau's imagination and memory, for the original state of reverie may well have been less exalted than this description suggests. (The account of the same episode in the *Confessions* is much more matter-of-fact than that of the fifth Promenade.) Even so, the later elaboration is in perfect accord with Rousseau's profound need to overcome the limitations of ordinary temporal and psychological experience; he seeks to become completely identified with a present which has all the fullness and none of the imperfections of everyday life.

The same fundamental concern is also apparent in another special mood described by Rousseau in the same work. In the second Promenade he relates how he was knocked unconscious by a large dog and how, on regaining his senses, his normal awareness of time and space suddenly gave way to a state of consciousness which excluded all pain (even though he had been badly injured) and all sense of personal identity. He was 'completely given to the present moment'. All normal feelings of pain, fear, or anxiety were absent; he did not know who or where he was. He felt a 'ravishing calm' different from anything he had ever experienced in the 'activity of known pleasures'. Unlike the other state of reverie, however, this complete identification with the present moment was accompanied by an equally remarkable loss of the normal awareness of space: 'It seemed as though I was filling all perceived objects with my light existence' (i. 1005). The distinction between self and non-self was completely abolished.

The episode with the dog also brings out another aspect of the peculiar fascination of this experience for Rousseau. The feeling of complete immediacy, of absolute identification with the present moment, gave him the illusion of a new birth. 'At that moment I was born to life' (i. 1005). In this way he could expel all thoughts of guilt and inadequacy from his existence; he was beginning life anew and rediscovering the pure innocence of rebirth. This desire had constantly preoccupied him in his early years and had expressed itself in various symbolic ways—in his predilection for the dawn and spring, moments when time and nature are reborn. Feeling himself to be at an absolute beginning, he was able to banish all disturbing thoughts from his mind; he had at last found refuge in a world from which even evil persecutors were excluded.

Nevertheless, Rousseau was aware of the precarious character of such experiences. Being intensely personal, a happiness of this kind needed an objective basis to give it stability and permanence. Unfortunately for Rousseau, the principle of order, which played such a prominent part in his philosophical system, was not adequate for this personal situation, because it tended to remain too remote from immediate experience to provide a satisfactory foundation for his daily life. Moreover, his physical decline no longer let him identify himself ecstatically with the order of physical nature and the spirit of the universal system. Since he was also cut off by universal hostility from participation in any kind of human society, the only order now available to him was of a spiritual sort. Yet even this spiritual order could be anticipated only in thought as existence in the next world: it was an object of hope and expectation rather than of immediate experience. He was, therefore, forced to seek another basis for his happiness—one that would be objective and yet form a part of his own being. He required something more durable than the transitory memories and fantasies of his day-dreams and, at the same time, more personal than the mere solidity of physical objects.

For a time, Rousseau hoped that the *Rêveries* he was composing would help him to bridge the gap between inner and outer worlds. For a man seeking happiness from his own resources, literary composition of a strictly personal nature would perhaps allow him to achieve some degree of self-sufficiency and independence since, by conversing with his own soul, he would be both subject and object, the author and the written word; the act of writing and the subsequent perusal of his own words would increase his happiness by letting him feel that he was both expressing and contemplating his own self—a self that was given objective embodiment through the medium of language. He hoped to discover that the reading of his own words would not only revive the pleasure he found in writing them, but also let him feel that he was in some sense communicating with his own inner being. 'The reading of them will recall my pleasure in writing them and thus reviving past time for me, will so to speak double my existence. In spite of men, I shall still know how to relish the charm of society and I shall live with my decrepit self in another age, as I should live with a friend less old' (i. 1001).

In spite of these early hopes Rousseau soon found that after they had been written down, his words lost their vitality and no longer formed part of his living substance. To have real meaning, literary activity would not only have to be constantly renewed but also limited to the memory of past happiness. Unfortunately the act of personal reflection which brought Rousseau comfort was also a source of torment, for it revived feelings of guilt and unworthiness as well as of happy fulfilment. By the time he began his seventh Promenade, he was already thinking of abandoning the project. He had found that another amusement, botany, was capable of providing him with greater satisfaction; not only did it replace the impersonal medium of the written word by nature's living objects, but it also relieved him of the necessity of reflection by allowing him to 'dream at his ease' and to let his imagination follow its natural bent; at times he could 'hover in the universe on the wings of imagination, in ecstasies which surpass all other joys'. To bring permanence and objectivity into this innocent pastime, Rousseau proposed to make a herbarium which would have the same function as his writings: it would serve as a diary of his expeditions. 'This herbarium is for me a diary of my botanizing which makes me begin them again with a fresh charm and produces the effect of an optical glass which would again depict them to my eyes' (i. 1073). Since botany involved the exploration of detailed aspects of the natural world, it did not arouse the deeper emotions associated with the contemplation of the universal system of nature *en masse*. The herbarium gave him quieter but more permanent contentment; since it represented the crystallization of memories and the impressions culled from his rambles through scenes of natural beauty, it allowed him to revive at will the pleasures of the past by the mere inspection of his botanical specimens. A particular attraction of this new hobby was that it enabled him to abandon himself to the feeling of his innocence; it was an immediate activity which also recalled his 'innocent pleasures' and let him enjoy them once again; in the presence of physical nature he could free himself from anxious thoughts by holding fast to the idea of his goodness and innocence. No doubt the herbarium also had its limitations, since the plants and flowers he collected soon became dead specimens and were transformed into mere objects of contemplation. Nevertheless, the herbarium could be constantly renewed and extended by fresh contact with living nature. More important still, the botanizing expeditions at last helped him to overcome all inner divisions and bridge the gap between himself and the external world.

In view of this, it is perhaps appropriate that the *Rêveries* should have remained unfinished. Rousseau ceased work on them a few weeks before his death. It is impossible to say whether this was a deliberate act of renunciation or a mere accidental cessation of his literary activity. The preference accorded to botany over writing in the seventh Promenade suggests that at the very end of his life Rousseau had decided to make anxious reflection yield to the reality of immediate experience.

Notes

1. On Rousseau's attitude towards his reader see R. J. Ellrich, *Rousseau and His Reader: the rhetorical situation of the major works* (Chapel Hill, University of North Carolina Press), 1969.

2. The expression is taken from Juvenal's *Satires*, iv. 91.

Conclusion

The starting-point of Rousseau's thought was a very radical criticism of contemporary civilization: he challenged some of the basic presuppositions of an age that prided itself on its 'philosophy', that is, its rational and enlightened view of man's place in the world. Far from treating modern culture as the culmination of a long process that had taken humanity from darkness to light, Rousseau considered it to be an unmistakable sign of corruption: intellectual achievement had been accompanied by moral decadence. In Rousseau's opinion, the basis of society was being undermined by false values. Although *philosophes* like Voltaire and Diderot made vigorous attacks upon contemporary social abuses, their main concern was with removing particular evils and not with disturbing the foundations of the existing social order. Because it was more general, Rousseau's criticism of society was also more radical: he believed that since the very basis of political and social life was unsound, it was necessary to expose the glaring inadequacy of attitudes which rested on opinion and prejudice rather than on moral and rational principles; the laws, for example, served only to help the strong and the rich against the poor and weak; religious institutions were primarily a source of intolerance and discord; the modern educational system produced nothing but artificial or distorted beings who bore little resemblance to true men.

Rousseau was not content to criticize existing evils: *Émile* and the *Contrat social* prove the earnestness of his efforts to find effective remedies. Because it was a question of establishing fundamental principles instead of dealing with merely peripheral issues, his first major task was to examine the nature of man and its place in the 'order of things'; he did not hesitate to call himself 'the portrayer of nature' and 'the historian of the human heart'. His constructive ideas were based on an assumption made by most of his contemporaries, namely, that there was a universal human nature, a definite essence of man; where he differed from other thinkers was in his conception of that essence and of the way in which it could be discovered. His rejection of traditional philosophical methods led him to adopt a new approach to human nature. Since history was the story of man's fall, and the present state of the world the consequence of his degradation, the meaning of his being could not be clarified by either a metaphysical or an empirical analysis of the historical situation, for such an approach would be either too abstract or too narrow to reveal the fundamental principles lying at the basis of human existence. Truth could not be reached in this way, because the very instrument on which it relied—reason and the other human powers associated with it—had been corrupted by the influence of society. Rousseau, therefore, had no 'philosophical method' in the strict sense of the term, for he did not develop a complex argument from certain clearly defined intellectual assumptions. Far from being a mere philosophical exercise, his first work was inspired by a sudden 'illumination' which represented the crystallization of deeply felt convictions rather than of clearly enunciated ideas. An aversion to contemporary society and culture that originated in a number of personal and general motives compelled him (in his own favourite phrase) 'to withdraw into himself' and seek 'the eternal principles written in the depth of his heart in indelible characters'.

As soon as these intuitively apprehended principles had been firmly established, Rousseau believed that it was possible to draw from them certain detailed conclusions concerning the human condition. If necessary, he was prepared to subject his principles to intellectual analysis and to set them out in technical language, as in the case of the *Contrat social*. Yet if the origin of his ideas could always be traced back to his own inner being, and if he refused to separate the two questions: 'What is truth?' and 'What am I?' he did not believe that the personal origin of truth would lead to mere subjectivism, since the life of the individual was bound up with that of other people. After seeking the truth in himself, the Savoyard priest urged his young friend to consult his own heart, for he would there discover principles valid for all men; the individual who learnt to know himself would also learn to know human nature. Moreover, in spite of his repudiation of contemporary philosophizing, Rousseau's early efforts to build 'a storehouse of ideas' show his willingness to relate his principles to a much wider cultural context than that of his own personal standpoint; he recognized that the most sincere and eager seeker of the truth had to scrutinize other thinkers' ideas in order to clarify and develop the universal implications of his own convictions.

In spite of the personal origin of Rousseau's ideas, there is, as earlier critics have pointed out, a strongly Platonizing element in his thought. If he denied the possibility of knowing the ultimate meaning of things by means of reason alone, he still believed that man could obtain some insight into the mystery of the creation when he responded to it with his whole being; such an attitude would enable him to discern a close spiritual affinity between the universal order and his own personal existence. Even though any purely rational attempt to explain the significance of this relationship was bound to fail, Rousseau acknowledged the value of giving it some kind of systematic expression; he always maintained, however, that formal philosophizing ought to be based on human need rather than on mere intellectual necessity. It was essential for the thinker to concentrate on what 'interested' him and 'what it was important for him to know'.

Although the didactic works show that Rousseau does not shun the wider metaphysical implications of his beliefs or their systematic enunciation, his principal concern is always with the nature of man. Admittedly, human nature is incomprehensible if it is considered apart from its place in the universal order, but man's attitude towards that order is also inseparable from his own needs as a free being. This means that human nature, in spite of its dependence on the order of nature, still has its own unique characteristics. Man is not a merely static being obeying fixed laws, like the physical world, for he chooses the meaning and direction of his life; it is his freedom which is his distinctive attribute. If his present unhappy condition is the result of a disastrous misuse of freedom, he can still do much to rectify the errors of the past; because he is free, he lives in the realm of possibility as well as actuality. At the same time, the possibilities open to him are not arbitrary or obscure, since there is a universal 'nature' capable of guiding him in his decisions. Rousseau's thought thus tries to reconcile the legitimate exercise of freedom with the valid demands of order.

If Rousseau's discussion of this problem leads him to present man with a vision of what he can become, he does not depict his future condition as a mere Utopia, but as an extension and expansion of his original being: the ideal always remains within the bounds of the possible. Consequently, the reality of immediate existence is transfigured by the ideal to which it aspires while still remaining faithful to its intrinsic being. This means, however, that Rousseau's habit of interpreting human existence in terms of its ideal possibilities excludes any serious interest in the analysis of facts for their own sake; the significance of what exists must be related to what it can become. In its broad metaphysical context this point of view presents no difficulty for Rousseau, since his conception of man as an evolving being is quite compatible with the idea of a well-ordered nature in which everything has its own appointed place; it is possible to allow each aspect of human nature to have its own characteristic perfection, its own mode of complete fulfilment, and yet acknowledge that every particular phase of existence has also to be linked up with a still higher mode of being, and, ultimately, with the perfection of the universal system.

In the most general meaning of the term, 'nature', as the universal order, constitutes a reality that already exists, while man's perfection, in the contemporary world, remains a mere possibility of his existence. Nevertheless, universal 'nature' also has an ideal aspect in so far as it is as yet inadequately known; to most men, who are members of an imperfect society, it must mean the rational and spiritual goal of their endeavours rather than the object of their immediate experience. At the same time, man's striving for fulfilment cannot ignore his dependence on his physical and psychological origins, or his 'nature' in a more restricted sense. 'Nature', therefore, has a static and dynamic—a factual and an ideal—aspect. Unwary readers are apt to be misled by Rousseau's habit of using the same term to denote the primordial aspects of a phenomenon as well as its intrinsic possibilities. Yet it is probably this fusion of realistic and idealistic elements which helps to give his philosophy its particular tone.

Although Rousseau is fully aware of the limitations and difficulties of the search for absolute self-realization, he is sometimes so completely captivated by his ideal that he overlooks the obstacles and imagines that perfection has already been achieved. Even though he knows that, in the present order of things, life is impossible without the support of virtue, he likes to think of happiness as a state in which man abandons himself effortlessly to the innate power of his goodness; the truly happy man has an overwhelming sense of personal harmony and plenitude and is completely identified with the 'feeling of his existence'. Yet Rousseau's occasional indulgence in this dream of static perfection never blinds him to the practical implications of his ideas and to the problem of giving them effective expression in the real world. It is interesting to observe, for example, how the final pages of *Émile* depict a curious fusion of idealism and reality: the 'golden age' and the 'earthly paradise' of perfect fulfilment are evoked in idyllic terms and yet with the admission that men's love of this ideal is not yet powerful enough to bring it into being. Émile, therefore, may have to leave his rural idyll in order to serve his country in 'the honourable function of citizen'. Although man is meant to be happy, the 'feeling of happiness crushes him, and he is not strong enough to bear it'; he needs virtue to make him capable of adapting himself to the reality of his immediate situation (cf. iv. 859–60).

Rousseau thus acknowledged that the entrancing ideal of complete self-realization could not ignore man's need to live in an organized society. Freedom is undoubtedly a unique and precious attribute, for it alone makes possible the fulfilment of personal existence, but it has to reckon with the practical implications of man's involvement in society. Just as primitive man has to respect the laws of nature, so must the citizen recognize the interdependence of freedom and political order: without the law there can be no equality of right, and without equality of right, there can be no true political freedom.

Nevertheless, the law cannot be accepted as something that simply exists, like the laws of nature, because it is a characteristic human achievement, the deliberate result of men's decision to live with one another in justice and equity. It is, therefore, necessary to combine a strong sense of personal responsibility with the acceptance of principles valid for all members of the community. If the laws of a sound political constitution guarantee each citizen's rights and protect him from oppression and exploitation, they also depend on his moral integrity and his willingness to put virtue above self-interest; only the man who has learnt to become 'master of himself' will become a worthy and responsible member of society.

If Rousseau occasionally indulges in his dream of spontaneously achieved perfection, his realism often impels him in the completely opposite direction of timid conservatism. The ardent advocate of 'natural religion', with its apparent exclusion of orthodoxy and revelation, is willing to allow the ruler of the State to determine the precise character of the national cult and require the citizens' obedience to it; the propounder of the democratic principle of the absolute sovereignty of the people is prepared to make considerable concessions to authority in order to avoid the revolution and internal discord he so strongly abhors, so that when he comes to imagine his ideal community—as in *La Nouvelle Héloïse*—it is not surprising to find him depicting it in paternalistic rather than egalitarian terms. Rousseau is by no means convinced that man will attain happiness without the help of guides and leaders, as is already apparent from his portrayal of Wolmar and the Lawgiver. Nevertheless, these guides are rarely invested with legal authority. They have to achieve their purpose by the sole influence of their personality and innate genius, and are intended to help man rather than to dominate him; they exist as means rather than ends.

Both the radical and the conservative aspects of Rousseau's thought owe a great deal to his overriding concern with unity. One of the most disastrous effects of modern society, according to Rousseau, has been to put man in conflict with himself and with his fellow men. The fulfilled individual—like the just and stable society—will have overcome the contradictions which are the greatest obstacle to happiness; he will be truly happy as soon as he has become himself in his essential unity. Likewise, citizens will not be at peace with one another until they are united by a common respect for the law, because only then will they feel free from possible subjection to another's will. Rousseau's concern with unity also explains his preference for small, self-sufficient States, which contain citizens united by their common desire for the well-being of the community. A truly unified society, like a truly unified individual, will have succeeded in combining the two principles of freedom and order.

However prominent it may be in Rousseau's thought, this preoccupation with unity, whether individual or social, is not always expressed with the same kind of emphasis. In *Émile* and the *Contrat social* Rousseau affirms that effective unity can be attained only by an effort of will, but he also tends, as we have seen, to treat happiness as a free and spontaneous expression of man's innate feelings. Although the principle of order embodied in the ideals of virtue and justice cannot be ignored in either personal or social life, for it lies at the very heart of the creation itself, true happiness consists of a joyous acquiescence in that order rather than of a voluntary adaptation to it. This explains why Rousseau, even when he is in his most austere mood and fiercely castigating the evils of contemporary society, cannot help casting a nostalgic glance at 'the simplicity of early times' when man was happy on 'a fine shore adorned by nature's hands alone'. Genuine happiness will be achieved only when the activity of the will gives way to the experience of innocence, simplicity, and goodness and when a new nature has overcome the limitations of the old. Yet it would probably be wrong to see this ideal as a contradictory element in Rousseau's didactic work, for he there acknowledges that until they reach this goal, men must continue to accept virtue and justice—rather than mere goodness—as the basis of their social existence; he never repudiates the need for moral principles, even though he sometimes likes to look beyond the limitations of the human situation to the paradise of perfect fulfilment.

Rousseau's philosophy is essentially optimistic. Since man's corruption has come from society and not from his own original nature, it has originated in weakness, blindness, and ignorance rather than in deliberate wickedness; humanity is faced with the drama of error, not the tragedy of guilt. It is on this central point that Rousseau is in accord with thinkers of the Enlightenment and in opposition to Christian tradition. Although he himself persists in claiming to be a 'Christian in the manner of Jesus Christ', he rejects the idea of sin, especially the theological doctrine of original sin; man has been corrupted by the historical and social process, but he has not been irremediably depraved. He can still hope to find salvation by his own efforts and attain happiness through the proper use of his own faculties; since nature itself can satisfy all his needs, he does not need to rely on the unpredictable operation of supernatural grace or the dogmas of a revealed religion. On this essential point Rousseau does not look back to Pascal or forward to Kierkegaard, but to the spirit of his own age.

If he is a man of the Enlightenment in his rejection of revelation, he none the less sees himself as an opponent of the *philosophes* in his zealous defence of the principles of natural religion. He believes that without religious principles, human existence remains narrow and incomplete, incapable of realizing its true possibilities. Rousseau is convinced that the materialism of the *philosophes* will mutilate human existence by depriving it of all idealism and by limiting it to the superficial domain of sense-experience. Religion, on the other hand, involves the expression of deep sensibility and feeling, as well as of reason and sensation. Rousseau's own works are intended to take men beyond the sterility of materialism and scepticism by reawakening them to the richness and abundance of their natural being, and to an awareness of their proper place in the universal system.

In view of the complexity of Rousseau's thought as a whole, it is not surprising that the particular nature of its appeal should have altered with the passing of time. To his own age, which had forgotten the meaning of simple humanity, Rousseau offered the hope of regeneration. He did not intend the impact of his work to be purely intellectual, for he urged men to go beyond the boundaries of reflection and abstract speculation to the renewal of their entire being. On the other hand, his criticism of contemporary thought was not meant to encourage a plunge into irrationalism: he wanted reason to function in harmony with sensibility and other human capacities. This harmonious development of the personality, however, could not be achieved until the basis of its existence had been re-examined, the source of authentic experience rediscovered; it was necessary to cut through the subtlety, artificiality, and corruption of existing society in order to find the simplicity, innocence, and plenitude of a new experience. As soon as he had fulfilled himself in this way, man would be like 'a new being recently come forth from nature's hands'; even though it was no longer possible for him to go back to the lost paradise of primitive innocence, he could still find happiness in the rediscovery of goodness and the experience of a second birth. It was Rousseau's constant emphasis upon the possibility of making a new beginning and of recovering lost purity that helps to explain his revitalizing influence upon an age that was beginning to grow tired of its intellectual sophistication; he held out the hope of a complete and unified personal existence, free from all inner conflict. No doubt his was far from being a lone voice, for the age of Enlightenment was already beginning to feel the influence of various 'pre-romantic' impulses which were making it react against excessive rationality and intellectualism, but Rousseau's literary genius enabled him to express his idealistic fervour in a particularly effective and urgent way; he made men more explicitly aware of their need for perfection and renewal and yet left them with a sense of their own personal reality.

In view of this, it is perhaps not surprising that Rousseau's political principles, with their somewhat austere character, as well as the rational, abstract manner of their presentation, should have made a more limited appeal to contemporary readers than his other ideas. Although they were clearly intended to be an essential part of his philosophy as a whole, in so far as they sought to reconcile freedom and social order, their close link with morality made them less immediately attractive than the ideas of *Émile* which traced the development of the individual from childhood to maturity: the portrayal of the happy individual was perhaps more easily appreciated than that of the virtuous State. Moreover, the influence of the *ancien régime* was still too strong to allow a radical reappraisal of the existing political order in the light of Rousseau's principles. It needed the upheaval of the French Revolution to stimulate enthusiastic interest in the *Contrat social*, and make its ideas seem relevant to the immediate historical situation.[1]

An adequate understanding of Rousseau's thought was certainly made more difficult by the posthumous publication of his personal writings with their portrayal of the lonely, persecuted, and misunderstood Jean-Jacques. Fascinated by the image of the good and innocent man of nature vilified by a wicked world, later generations exaggerated the individualism of Rousseau's philosophical outlook and ignored his repeated stress on the importance of order at every level of human experience. In spite of important links between the two, it is misleading to see the formal works in the sole perspective of the personal ones, for the latter were written by a man who considered himself to be exceptional; what appears in the didactic works as a goal that can be reached only after a long and arduous experience of all the complexities of the human condition, becomes in the personal writings an ideal deserving of immediate fulfilment by the good and innocent Jean-Jacques. Nevertheless, the earlier stress on unity reappears in the last works with Rousseau's desire for perfect inner consistency and plenitude. There is also the same absence of tragic dimension: like man himself, Jean-Jacques must be absolved from the responsibility of all guilt and wickedness, which are henceforth attributed to a typical element of contemporary society—his ruthless persecutors.

Yet because Rousseau's yearning for the unity of absolute fulfilment could not overcome anxious self-questioning, his efforts to stabilize the antithesis between the good Jean-Jacques and his wicked enemies made him rely more and more upon his own inner resources as a means of escaping from the tormenting presence of a hostile world; he was led to explore new modes of consciousness and to seek a state of being that would 'deliver him from the anxiety of hope'. Although he never doubted the ultimate basis of his didactic writings—indeed, his very last work categorically affirmed his refusal to re-examine questions which he had already answered to the best of his ability when he was in full possession of his powers—the deepening of his inner life developed his preoccupation with hitherto neglected aspects of human existence; the mood of reverie, for example, seemed to liberate him from the normal restrictions of time and space by allowing him to live in an 'eternal present' and enjoy a self-sufficient 'feeling of existence'; at other times the affective power of memory as well as his emotional and spiritual aspirations modified his attitude towards the physical world, and led him to a highly personal feeling for nature. In this way, Rousseau opened up vistas which a later Romantic generation accepted as part of its own particular world. Yet, as the preceding pages have attempted to show, this was only one facet of a complex personality which strove constantly to pass beyond the limitations of solitude and establish a harmonious relationship between human nature and the universal system of which it formed part.

Note

1. Cf. Joan McDonald, *Rousseau and the French Revolution, 1762–1791* (London, 1965).

Select Bibliography

WORKS AND CORRESPONDENCE

Jean-Jacques Rousseau: *Oeuvres complètes*, ed. B. Gagnebin and M. Raymond, Paris, 1959–70, vol. i (*Confessions et autres textes autobiographiques*); vol. ii (*La Nouvelle Héloïse: théâtre: poésies*); vol. iii (*Du Contrat social: écrits politiques*); vol. iv (*Émile: éducation: morale: botanique*). (Vol. v has yet to be published.)

The following works have not yet been included in the above edition:
Lettre à d'Alembert sur les spectacles, ed. M. Fuchs, Geneva, 1948.
Essai sur l'origine des langues, ed. C. Porset, Bordeaux, 1968.

English editions of the French text of the collected political and religious writings are:
Political Writings of J.-J. Rousseau, ed. C. E. Vaughan, 2 vols., Cambridge, 1915.
Rousseau's Religious Writings, ed. R. Grimsley, Oxford, 1970.

There are two English editions of the *Contrat social*:
Du Contrat social, ou principes du droit politique, ed. C. E. Vaughan, Manchester, 1918.
Du Contrat social, edited, with an introduction and notes, by R. Grimsley, Oxford, 1972.

Two useful translations are:
The Social Contract and Discourses, trans. G. D. H. Cole (Everyman's Library), London, 1913.

The Social Contract, trans. M. Cranston (Penguin Books), Harmonds-
worth, 1968.

The definitive edition of the correspondence, now in course of publication,
is:
Correspondance complète de Jean-Jacques Rousseau, ed. R. A. Leigh,
Geneva, 1957–. (16 vols. so far published.)

For the period not yet available in the above edition:
Correspondance générale de J.-J. Rousseau, ed. T. Dufour, and P.-P. Plan,
20 vols., Paris, 1924–34.

A critical survey of Rousseau studies is to be found in an excellent
chapter, 'On reading Rousseau', in Peter Gay's *The Party of Humanity:
Studies in the French Enlightenment* (London, 1964) and in the remark-
able bibliographical essay appended to the same author's important work,
The Enlightenment: An Interpretation (2 vols., London, 1966–70, esp.
ii. 694–700). (The same volume also contains a lively chapter on Rousseau.)
For a comprehensive survey of earlier studies on Rousseau, Albert Schinz's
État présent des travaux sur J.-J. Rousseau (Paris, 1941) is still valuable.

Bibliographical details of all important studies on Rousseau, as well as
original articles, are to be found in the *Annales de la société Jean-Jacques
Rousseau* (Geneva, 1905 onwards).

BOOKS ON ROUSSEAU

For the biography of Rousseau:
GREEN, F. C., *Jean-Jacques Rousseau*, Cambridge, 1955.
GUÉHENNO, J., *Jean-Jacques Rousseau*: translated by J. and D. Weight-
man. 2 vols., London, 1966 (The original French edition was entitled,
Jean-Jacques, 3 vols., Paris, 1940–52, and subsequently published in 2
vols. as *Jean-Jacques, Histoire d'une conscience*, Paris, 1962.)
CROCKER, L. G., *J.-J. Rousseau: The Quest: 1712–1758*, New York,
1968.

For Rousseau's Genevan background:
VALLETTE, G., *Jean-Jacques Rousseau genevois*, Paris, 1908.
SPINK, J. S., *Rousseau et Genève*, Paris, 1934.

For Rousseau's psychology and personal development:
PROAL, L., *La Psychologie de J.-J. Rousseau*, Paris, 1930.
GRIMSLEY, R., *Jean-Jacques Rousseau, a Study in Self-Awareness*, Car-
diff, 1961 (2nd revised edition, 1969).
RAYMOND, M., *Rousseau, la quête de soi et la rêverie*, Paris, 1962.

Useful general introductions:

BROOME, J. H., *Rousseau: A Study of his Thought*, London, 1963.

CASSIRER, E., *The Question of Jean-Jacques Rousseau*, trans. P. Gay, New York, 1962.

MAY, G., *Rousseau par lui-même*, Paris, 1961.

LAUNAY, M., *Rousseau*, Paris, 1968 (brief study with extracts).

MORNET, D., *Rousseau, l'homme et l'œuvre*, Paris, 1950.

WRIGHT, E. H., *The Meaning of Rousseau*, Oxford, 1929.

Two outstanding studies of Rousseau's works are:

BURGELIN, P., *La Philosophie de l'existence de J.-J. Rousseau*, Paris, 1950.

STAROBINSKI, J., *Jean-Jacques Rousseau, la transparence et l'obstacle (suivi de sept essais sur Rousseau)*, Paris, 1970.

On Rousseau's early works:

EINAUDI, M., *The Early Rousseau*, New York, 1967.

For the chronological development of Rousseau's thought and extended summaries of the main works:

HENDEL, C. W., *Jean-Jacques Rousseau*, 2 vols., Oxford, 1934. (Republished with new preface, New York, 1962.)

For Rousseau's view of reason:

DERATHÉ, R., *Le Rationalisme de Jean-Jacques Rousseau*, Paris, 1948.

On Rousseau's religion:

MASSON, P. M., *La Religion de J.-J. Rousseau*, 3 vols., Paris, 1916.

GRIMSLEY, R., *Rousseau and the Religious Quest*, Oxford, 1968.

On Rousseau's political views:

CHAPMAN, J. W., *Rousseau, totalitarian or liberal?*, New York, 1956.

COBBAN, A., *Rousseau and the Modern State*, London, 1934 (2nd revised edition, 1964).

CROCKER, L. G., *Rousseau's Social Contract: an Interpretive Essay*, Cleveland, 1968.

DERATHÉ, R., *Rousseau et la science politique de son temps*, Paris, 1950.

LAUNAY, M., *J.-J. Rousseau: écrivain politique, 1712–62*, Grenoble, 1971.

MASTERS, R. D., *The Political Philosophy of Rousseau*, Princeton, 1968.

SHKLAR, J. N., *Men and Citizens; a Study of Rousseau's Social Theory*, Cambridge, 1969.

Three volumes devoted exclusively to Rousseau's political views are:

Études sur le Contrat social de Jean-Jacques Rousseau. Actes de journées d'étude organisées à Dijon, Paris, 1964.

Annales de philosophie politique, 5 (1965): *Rousseau et la philosophie politique*.

Annales de la société Jean-Jacques Rousseau, 35 (1959–62): *Entretiens sur Jean-Jacques Rousseau*.

Rousseau's aesthetic views have not been given separate treatment. Useful indications are to be found in Michel Launay's introduction mentioned above. Separate studies of his musical theories:

JANSEN, A., *Jean-Jacques Rousseau als Musiker*, Berlin, 1884.

POUGIN, A., *J.-J. Rousseau musicien*, Paris, 1940.

TIERSOT, J., *Jean-Jacques Rousseau*, Paris, 1920.

On Rousseau's attitude towards his reader:

ELLRICH, R. J., *Rousseau and his reader: the rhetorical situation of the major works*, Chapel Hill, N.G., 1969.

Index